CIRCUIT
TRAINING
FOR ALL SPORTS

22.00

CIRCUIT TRAINING FOR ALL SPORTS

Methodology of effective fitness training

Written by **Manfred Scholich, PhD**

Edited by **Peter Klavora, PhD**
School of Physical and Health Education
University of Toronto

Sport Books Publisher Toronto

Translation by Linda Paul

Canadian Cataloguing in Publication Data

Scholich, Manfred.
  Circuit training for all sports

1st Canadian ed.
Translation of: Kreistraining.
Bibliography: p.
ISBN 0-920905-04-8

1. Circuit Training. I. Klavora, Peter
II. Title.

GV462.S613 1990 613.7'1 C86-095081-6

Distribution worldwide by
Sport Books Publisher
278 Robert Street
Toronto, Ontario M5S 2K8
Canada

Printed in the United States

Contents

Preface

Efficient and standard forms of training are necessary in physical education programs and competitive sports training. Circuit training has proved an especially effective instrument for this purpose. Introduced at the University of Leeds in the late fifties, circuit training is a systematic and controlled way of conditioning designed to improve general and specific fitness.

The original concept has undergone various changes affecting all areas of physical fitness and sport. Intensive research over the past thirty years at the School of Physical Education and Sport, University of Leipzig, has resulted in the development of training methods that form the basis for the circuit training programs and their many variations described in this book. In addition, this research has (1) shown positive training effect in all trainees, regardless of age, sex, and ability, and (2) confirmed the usefulness of taking heart rate measurements by trainees before and after training as a criterion of cardiovascular fitness.

Circuit training is a form of training that is enjoyable, measurable, and generates immediate positive changes in all fitness components. The intensity and vigor of circuit training exercises challenge and motivate the performer, thus making conditioning fun through competition against teammates and against time.

In addition to explaining the methodology and principles of circuit training, this book presents over thirty sample circuit training programs designed for general and sport-specific training. These programs can be easily modified and adapted to suit the available equipment, space, and most important, the needs of trainees. Indeed, coaches and instructors are encouraged to develop the methods presented in this book further. *Editor*

1 The Concept of General and Sport Specific Fitness

The health, *joie de vivre,* and creativity of a well developed personality depend to a great degree upon general physical fitness levels. Fitness is the functional readiness and level of effectiveness required and/or desired by each athlete, depending on the level of development of physical skills and capacities, as well as of intellectual and emotional abilities, character traits, behaviour, and attitudes.

General physical fitness forms the basis for sport-specific fitness and is ultimately related to it. High levels of general physical fitness constitute important prerequisites for the effective and optimum development of sport-specific fitness. Conversely, improvements in sport-specific fitness by means of training have a positive effect on the improvement of general physical fitness. Furthermore, both develop on the basis of the highly specific laws or rules governing exercise.

The development of general physical and sport-specific fitness is a process that is experienced by the athlete's entire personality and that must be mastered. The development process, in other words, involves the development of the whole personality as it is reflected in the continuous improvement of fitness abilities. Athletes who seek such an improvement must pay attention to the development of:

- abilities related to fitness and coördination,
- motor-technical skills,
- tactical abilities,
- intellectual abilities,
- knowledge and experience, and
- readiness to apply themselves.

A complex development of various physical abilities and skills is achieved by varying the stress levels that a training load imposes upon the athlete. This is accomplished by altering the relationship between the training components, intensity, volume, density, and duration of exercise. (These components are defined and discussed in the next chapter.)

In general and sport-specific fitness training, it is not only the quantity of how much is accomplished during the exercise that counts, but also the *quality* of the exercise execution. To develop fitness skills to optimum levels, athletes must master the necessary techniques and execute the exercises correctly, performing all the required movements. This should help them develop coordination and motor-technical skills.

The collective experience of coaches and instructors, as well as research in exercise physiology on the effective development of individual fitness abilities, is vital for formulating training principles in general and for defining the variations inherent in circuit training in particular. The characteristics of various fitness abilities (strength, speed, endurance) can also be seen as providing the basis for optimal loading and determining an optimal relationship between exercise and recovery, thereby for formulating a methodical and well-regulated system of training through circuit training.

Fitness abilities developed through circuit training presented in this book are mainly related to muscular strength and its components, the maximal strength, power, muscular endurance, and cardiovascular conditioning or aerobic endurance.

1.1   Maximal Strength

Maximal strength is the ability of the athlete to perform maximal voluntary muscular contractions in order to overcome powerful external resistances. It is the greatest force an athlete can exert for a given contraction of muscles, that is, the highest load the athlete can lift in one attempt. The highest absolute strength is necessary for such activities as weightlifting, wrestling, shotput, hammer throw, and so on. Its importance for an athletic performance diminishes as the resistance that must be overcome in competition is reduced and as the period of competition increases.

Muscle strength is dependent upon muscle size. The larger the muscle, the stronger it is. Muscle size can be enlarged by strenuous exercise using resistance of 90-100% of maximal strength capacity. It is possible to maintain the strength required to hold one's own body weight or to perform movements with maximal resistance generally only for a short period of time, since the body is not able to provide an adequate supply of oxygen while the high application of strength per unit of time lasts. For this reason, the body must sometimes go into a period of *oxygen debt*. There is a direct relationship between the volume and the duration of strength applied and the oxygen debt (see Figure 1 on p. 19). The oxygen debt is particularly high when a great deal of strength is exerted against a strong external resistance, depending on the number of repetitions (such as in strength exercises) to be made, as well as for speed or distance to be run. The working muscles are placed under *anaerobic* conditions (low in oxygen), the result of high muscle use, thereby taxing them to the maximum. According to research (16, 21), this condition is conducive to muscle growth. Oxygen deficiency is accompanied by high levels of lactic acid concentration and other waste products which cause rapid local (muscle) and central (nervous) fatigue. The physiological ability to work is thus sharply reduced. It is important, therefore, that following every period of strenuous activity (using resistance of 90-100% of maximal performance ability) recovery breaks be provided that allow for a return to activity. According to experimental results (16), the rest should be relatively long, from 3-5 minutes, depending on the type and nature of the exercise, since during this time it is possible to compensate for deficiencies in oxygen and energy supply. The number of repetitions in maximal strength training is relatively very low.

1.2   Power

Power, often referred as *speed-strength,* is the ability of the athlete to overcome external resistance by developing a high rate of muscular contraction. The ability of power is decisive in the speed of execution of individual movements performed in acyclic activities, for example, in field events such as throwing, high- or long-jumps. It is also important for the achievement of a high push-off, throw or take-off velocity in games, for the mastering of quick movement in individual activities, for acceleration in sprinting and skating, as well as for fast starts and accelerations in rowing and similar events.

To develop power effectively, exercise requirements should be such that an increase of fatigue is avoided. The number of times an exercise is repeated for each series, depending on strength requirements, is only 4 to 8 for *acyclic movements* (one motor action is comprises of several intricate but qualitatively different movements, such as boxing, wrestling, diving, and shot putting); for *cyclic movements* (same motor action as swimming, running, cycling is repeated over and over) it is 6 to 20. Exercise pace is brisk. Movement rate has to be at least equal to competition-specific movement rate.

The development of power requires sub-maximal but explosive force or strength application within the range of 75-90% of the maximal performance capacity. The onset of fatigue is thus sharply increased with repeated power loadings. A recovery break of 90-240 seconds is needed to ensure optimum recovery (16).

1.3   Muscular Endurance

Muscular endurance or *strength endurance* is the ability of an athlete to resist fatigue in strength performance of longer duration. It determines performances in those endurance activities where exceptional resistance must be overcome over relatively longer periods of time, such as in rowing, swimming, and cross-country skiing.

Muscular endurance is also important in such predominantly acyclic activities where high demands are placed on strength and endurance as in gymnastics, wrestling, boxing, downhill skiing, and most games.

As a rule, muscular endurance is an integral component of all forms of *specific endurance* that include *power endurance* (also referred to as *speed endurance*) and to short, medium, or longer endurance ability. Muscular endurance is thus an integral component of all forms of *specific endurance*. In other words, the level of development of specific endurance and that of muscular endurance are mutually dependent. The development and improvement of muscular endurance is therefore specific, and depends upon:

• the exercises chosen (whether with acyclic or cyclic movements),
• the duration of exercise,
• the intensity of exercise, and
• the density of exercise.

Within the framework of general and sport-specific fitness training, strength exercises with acyclic movement sequences with repetitions normally retain a cyclical character.

Exercise duration, which is the total time of the various repetitions of acyclic movements at a certain tempo, causes metabolic reactions to ensure energy is directed to the working muscles. These reactions in turn rigorously reinforce the muscular endurance performance, just as they also assist power endurance ability and short, medium, and longer endurance ability in the case of cyclic movements. The bulk of the energy in training for muscular endurance is provided under either anaerobic or aerobic conditions (see Figure 1 on p. 19) depending on the intensity of exercise (high, medium, or low).

The relatively non-specific nature of the autonomic nervous system makes it possible to begin preparing the body immediately for specific and performance-governed metabolic responses with cyclic or acyclic movements, through generally developed exercises.

For the development and improvement of muscular endurance, the following rules apply (depending on the interrelationship between the training components, the intensity, volume, duration, and density):

- Following strenuous periods of exertion at approximately 70-90% of maximal performance capacity, with 6-12 repetitions per series, and at a brisk tempo, an incomplete recovery from 60-180 seconds causes muscular with a high strength component to develop.

- Following moderate periods of exertion at around 50-70% of maximal performance capacity, with approximately 10-30 repetitions per series, a relatively short incomplete recovery of 30-120 seconds is sufficient for restoring performance ability. This type of training develops muscular endurance with a moderate strength component (24).

- Following low to moderate exertion at approximately 40-60% of maximal performance capacity, the exercising can be carried out continuously without any interruption. This type of muscular endurance training generates only a weak strength component.

If exertion is low during exercising (40-60%), any particular exercise may last for a long period of time (for example, jogging). Varied exercises may also be performed, each with relatively few repetitions (constantly varied and without stopping), lasting for a total of 10 minutes and up, to 45 minutes. Although, within the framework of general fitness training, anywhere from 6 to 18 different strength exercises may be performed one after the other in a training program, the exercise effect is mainly intended for improving general endurance.

Fatigue during this period is not governed by high oxygen deficiencies. Such a deficiency is almost insignificant here, since with low exertion during exercises physiological activity is carried out under aerobic conditions; that is, oxygen intake for conversion into energy equals oxygen consumption or needs. For such aerobic activity, the criterion should be, that, after initial quick jumps, the pulse rate stabilizes and remains constant. Depending on training and physical condition of the performer, pulse rate is at least 150 beats per minute and should not exceed 200 beats per minute.

An incomplete recovery which is typically used between sets following strenuous or moderate periods of exertion refers to the time needed for an athlete's partial recovery. During this time the recovery process is particularly rapid. The pulse rate drops from around 180 to 200 beats/min to around 120 to 140 beats/min. A fresh loading can be started once this partial recovery has been attained.

1.4   Cardiovascular Fitness

Cardiovascular fitness or *aerobic endurance* (also refered as *general endurance*) is the ability to produce new energy through an improved delivery of oxygen to the working muscles. Cardiovascular endurance is needed for exertions over relatively longer time periods regardless of the activity. It is intimately related to muscular endurance as the working muscles rely on oxygen supply sent by the heart, delivered via the blood, and "burned" within the muscles. Many types of circuit training designed to develop muscular endurance (notably circuit training based on the endurance and the extensive internal methods) generate a significant training effect upon the development of cardiovascular endurance as well. The major improvements related to the cardiovascular endurance are in the following biological systems and functions: lower resting and submaximal workload heart rate, greater maximal cardio output, greater maximal stroke volume, greater lung-ventilation efficiency, greater maximal oxygen consumption, capacity for greater oxygen debt, and greater capacity to recover.

2 Basic Principles of Sports Training

2.1 The Nature of Athlete's Adaptation to Training

In training theory it is generally customary to express the amount of activity which affects the body through exercising as the relationship between the *intensity* and *volume* of physical exercise. Intensity is defined as the application of strength within a certain period of time, and volume to be the number of repetitions or the duration of the exercise. The quantitative determination of the *external loading* (i.e., the total training load performed by the athlete) by intensity and volume enables the establishment of the nature and degree of *internal loading* as experienced by the athlete.

The purpose of this section is (1) to illustrate the nature and level of the athlete's internal loading as an expression of the interrelationship between intensity and volume of exercise; and (2) to explain the stimulation and the athlete's adaptation to exercise.

2.1.1 Stimulation and Athlete's Adaptation to Exercise

The ability of all living organisms to respond to changes in their environment by various changes in their own state and activity is called *sensitivity.* The agents that bring about changes in the state of living organisms are called *stimuli,* and their effect, which brings about a specific change in living organisms, is called *stimulation.*

Every living organism can be exposed to stimuli in the form of any physical, chemical (or a combination of the two) changes in the environment. When they reach a certain intensity, stimuli bring about certain changes in living organisms, which can be detected under experimental conditions, although often, in the case of skeletal muscle contraction for example, they can be observed without the assistance of special apparatus. The minimal intensity of the agent, sufficient enough to provoke a stimulation, is known as the *stimulus threshold.*

Each stimulus causes a change in metabolic activity - the most elementary response of living organisms to stimulation. At the same time, various types of tissue respond with specific reactions when they are subjected to a stimulus of a certain strength. A muscle, for example, responds to a stimulus with metabolic changes, which in turn cause the specific response of a muscle, i.e., the muscle contracts.

The response characteristic of each tissue (e.g., muscular, glandular, and nervous tissue), which is determined by its morphological and functional characteristics and which represents only a specific activity for each kind of tissue, is referred to as *excitation.* The capacity of tissue for specialized responses, which it expresses in the event of excitation in the form of a specific activity, is known as *excitability.* And finally, the agent's stimulus strength, which causes tissue reaction, plays a decisive role, since the specialized tissues react differently to specific stimuli intensities.

Stimuli of specific intensities that exceed the stimulus threshold excite the muscular tissue, which reacts by contracting. As a rule, the contraction of the skeletal muscles functions in accordance with the physical law of work, which states that *work = force x distance.* The magnitude of any muscular action is expressed by the formula: *muscular action = weight lifted x height of lift.* The height to which the weight is lifted is directly related to the intensity of the stimulus or stimulus strength, and increases with the strength of the stimulus. A strong stimulus exceeds the threshold for all muscle fibres, whereas a weak stimulus causes only a minor number of muscle fibres to contract. This muscular action is expressed in kgm. If time is added to these factors, we speak of *performance,* which is expressed in kgm/s.

2.1.2   Athlete's External and Internal Training Load

The athlete's ability to adapt physiologically to training stimuli corresponds to the level of demands or exertion (11). The exertion level or external loading can be quantitatively determined by adding the amount of external work per training unit, day, microcycle, and macrocycle. It can also be objectively estimated by using the following measurable parameters that constitute the external loading:

• intensity, volume, duration, and density of the exercise or loading,
• frequency of training,
• nature of physical exercises (degree of exertion, level of difficulty),
• demands made in the correct execution of the exercises, and
• intellectual demands for solving tactical problems.

When athletes exercise using the prescribed training program (external loading), internal demands are made. In other words, athletes experience the so-called *internal loading* which express their physical and psychological fatigue. An exact assessment of the degree of internal loading or exertion is extremely difficult to make without elaborate physiological tests. Furthermore, the same external loading makes varied internal demands across different athletes. It is also influenced by such factors as the weather, facilities, the calibre of competition, and the like.

It is therefore difficult to estimate internal work levels. However, an athlete's reactions and behaviour give the coach some indication of these conditions. These may be:

• manner in which the load is tackled,
• changes in mood (before and after exercising),
• readiness to execute exercises and sequences immediately,
• externally visible signs, such as reddening, paleness, sweating,
• the manner in which the athlete accepts and copes with performance changes in training,
• self-assessment of how an athlete experiences the training load, and
• changes in pulse rate before and after exercising (giving rough estimate of an athlete's work and recovery ability).

It is possible for the exercise physiologist to assess more objectively the type and level of internal loading by carrying out several tests that evaluate pulse rate changes, cardiac output per minute, oxygen consumption, oxygen pulse, lactic acid concentration, and other metabolic parameters. These tests require sophisticated laboratory equipment. On the other hand, pulse rate measurements before, during, and after training are easy to determine and should become a routine in every training environment.

2.1.3   The Athlete's Physiological Responses
to Intensity of Training

Circulation changes dramatically in accordance with changes in demands due to exercise. The physiological processes that cause these changes in the circulatory system belong to *circulatory or cardiovascular regulation*. The overwhelming importance of the regulation of cardiac action becomes evident from the fact that the quantity of the cardiac output may increase from 4-6 litres at complete rest to 20-35 litres during vigorous muscular activity. This is effected by an increase in the cardiac output of the left heart from 40-70 to 100-180 ml and that of the pulse rate from 60-70 to 180-240 beats/min (2).

The relationship between the amount of oxygen required and work intensity is shown in Figure 1. At the beginning of each phase of activity, there is an oxygen deficiency (oxygen debt) in the muscle. As soon as the amount of oxygen brought to the muscle within a certain

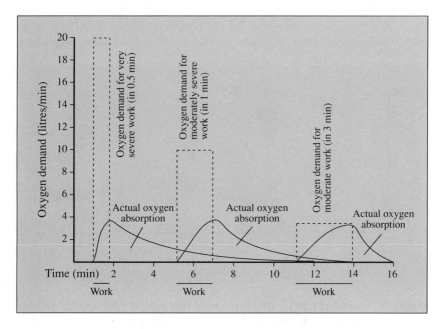

Figure 1   The relationship between oxygen demand and work intensity.

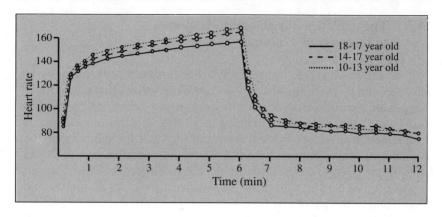

Figure 2   Heart rate in 10-19 year old males (n = 220) tested during a 6-min performance at 1 W/kg body weight at the hand crank ergometer, with a recovery phase lasting 6 min (19).

amount of time is sufficient for oxidation of all the lactic acid and other, partially oxidized anaerobic metabolic products that have been accumulated, metabolic activity reaches a stable state. The surplus of

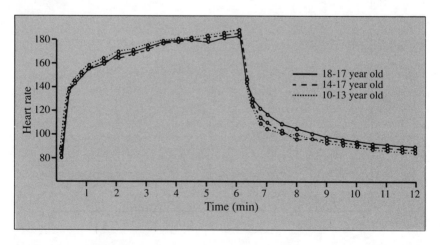

Figure 3   Heart rate of 10-19 year old males (n = 196) tested during a performance at 2 W/kg body weight over 6 min at the hand crank ergometer, with a recovery phase lasting 6 min (19).

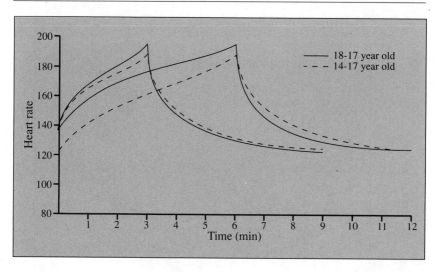

Figure 4   Heart rate comparison of 12-19 year old (n=160) and 20-
30 year old (n=100) subjects during and after a 3-min and
6-min maximal performance at the hand crank ergometer.
Exercise heart rate of the younger population is slightly
higher than that of the adults. After a recovery phase of 6
min the younger performers and the adults achieve the
same heart rate (approx. 100). This indicates an equal
ability for a recovery of two test groups following maximal
performance.

anaerobic waste products, which build up when activity begins (and
oxygen supply is lower than the oxygen requirement), is eliminated by
oxidation during the rest period, after work has stopped (15). Figure 1
shows the time required to eliminate oxygen debt during rest periods
is shorter for work at moderate intensity than it is for work at severe
intensity.

Figures 2 to 4 demonstrate the pulse rates in several groups of subjects as a function of intensity of exercise and the recovery process.
These diagrams also show that there are no significant differences in
exercise and recovery pulse rates among 10-19 year-old and 20-30
year-old subjects. The pulse rates of adolescents during a similar exercise are slightly higher than those of an adult subject performing the
same load per kg of body weight (19). This is not true, however, when

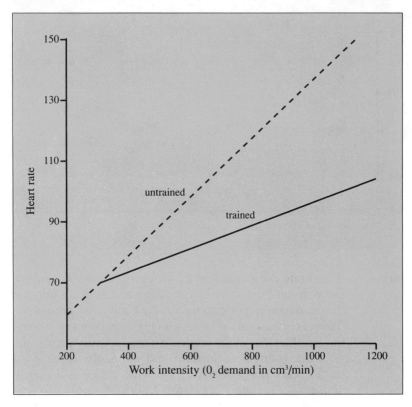

Figure 5   Oxygen demand and heart rates of trained and untrained
                  subjects as a function of intensity of exercise. After a
                  longer training period a drop in the pulse at constant
                  performance levels is a symptom of adaptation. Investiga-
                  tions have shown that children and youth adapt in ways
                  similar to adults.

those in training and those who are not are required to perform basi-
cally the same exercise (Figure 5). As work is increased per unit of
time, oxygen requirements continuously increase. Among less fit,
untrained subjects, the increase in heart rate is significantly higher
during periods of relatively similar activity in order to meet increasing
oxygen demands than the heart rate of more trained subjects (2).
    Pulse rates of 180-200 beats/min show clearly that the training load

has been assessed correctly. At this stage the cardiovascular system still works economically, although the metabolism has already undergone significant changes. Should the pulse rate climb above 200 beats/min, *minute volume rate* drops in spite of higher pulse rates; cardiac and circulatory activity then becomes uneconomical. *A diminished pulse rate at a relatively constant loading can therefore be regarded as a criterion of successful adaptation and as an indicator for an improved level of cardiovascular fitness or aerobic endurance .* This form of adaptation is proof of *economy* in the vital biological functional systems.

The findings from physiology and training research (10, 16, 19) form the basis for the development of four basic training methods presented in section 2.3. The methods were developed on the basis of differentiation between intensity and volume of exercise, and thus reflect the various relationships between loading and recovery. For this reason, then, they are also referred to as the "training load methods."

2.2   The Components of Training

In order to achieve the desired effect for a particular phase of training, a coach must use various training methods. The application of training methods permits coaches to plan, set, and to control the training program of athletes. Training methods also allow the instructors and coaches to quantify and assess the external load of a training unit and its parts in order to develop, stabilize, or maintain general and specific fitness of the athlete.

Training methods are based on two major components of training, the intensity of training and the volume of training. These components are further broken down into four subcomponents: the stimulus strength of exercise and the stimulus density of exercise are the subcomponents of intensity; the stimulus volume of exercise and the stimulus duration of exercise form the subcomponents of the volume of training. This breakdown makes it possible to accurately quantify the external loading by using various units of measurements. This allows an accurate gradation of the external load of training which in turn affects the internal load of the athlete and brings about a change in its quality. This facilitates the planning process of training and the evaluation of its effects.

2.2.1   Stimulus Intensity of Exercise

The stimulus intensity of exercise is the most important element of the intensity of training component with which the physical exercises are executed. Generally, it characterizes the degree of applied strength required per unit of time. The degree of stimulation intensity of exercise is measured in various units of measurement depending on the type of activity, as follows:

- Metre per second (m/s) and kilometre per hour (km/h) for cyclic activities, such as running, swimming, cross-country skiing, speed skating, cycling, rowing, and so on. These measurements represent the distance covered within a unit of time.

- Kilograms (kg), kilograms-metre (kgm) or kilograms-metre per second (kgm/s) for strength exercises, such as weightlifting, resistance training using dumbbells, barbells, and so on. These measurements represent the magnitude of an external resistance to be overcome, withstood or yielded to.

- Rate per unit of time for acyclic activities, such as gymnastics, figure skating, diving, ski jumping, ball games, and so on. This measurement represents the frequency or number of repetitions of the movement per unit of time.

- Metres (m) and centimetres (cm) for acyclic activities, such as shot-putting, long and high jumping, throwing and so on. These measurements represent the achieved length or height.

A 100 per cent performance is the personal best performance of an athlete when converted to the units of measurement described above. The stimulus intensity of a physical exercise expressed as a percentage will always represent the necessary expenditure of effort in comparison with the expenditure of effort necessary for achieving a best personal performance. Thus, the 100 per cent performance of an athlete becomes the staring point for defining the various ranges of relative intensities used in planning of training. It also makes comparisons of performance within the same intensity ranges across different athletes possible.

2.2.2   Stimulus Density of Exercise

The stimulus density of exercise refers to the relationship between the phases of work and rest during training. It also represents the relationship between effective exercising time and total training time. Athletes cannot work continuously without a break throughout a training session unless the intensity of exercise is relatively very low. Repeated application or maximal strength are simply not feasible until after an optimal recovery period. Generally, the lower the intensity of exercise per unit of time the shorter the rest periods required by the working athlete. Conversely, the higher the intensity of exercise per unit of time the longer the rest periods that must be scheduled. The length of the rest interval also depends upon the athlete's training status, the phase of training, and the training goals to be achieved within a particular training phase. The athlete's heart rate is normally used for determining the length of rest between individual sets and or series of exercises. A medium to sub-maximal training load generates heart rates in excess of 180 beats/min. Depending upon the fitness level of the athlete, after an incomplete recovery period of about 30 to 180 seconds, the pulse rate may drop to about 140 to 120 beats/min, at which point, according to research in exercise physiology (24), the athlete can resume exercising. An optimal load density prevents premature fatigue of the athlete, thus ensuring (a) the mastery of a high volume of training; (b) adherence to the desired intensity of training; and (c) the quality of movement which is given for the activity or exercise.

In general, training methods designed to improve endurance require relatively short rests when the intensity of exercise is relatively low. Training methods designed to improve speed and power require exercising at relatively high intensity levels with extended rest intervals to allow almost complete recovery.

2.2.3   The Volume of Exercise

Volume of training is one of the most important components of training. Under normal circumstances, it must continuously increase from year to year as the athlete's standard of performance rises. The term refers to the sum total of work performed during a training session or phase of training and is measured in various units depending upon the type of activity. In cyclic movements (running, swimming, rowing, and so on), the total distance (in metres or kilometres) in one run or several runs represents the volume of training. In acyclic movements (throwing, shotputting, jumping, and other technical events), the volume is represented by the total number of successful or unsuccessful repetitions or attempts made at a particular height, distance, and so on, during a training session. For example, a high-jumper may succeed ten times at 1.90 m height and six times at 2.00 m height, whereas at 2.05 m there were three unsuccessful attempts. The volume of training, i.e., the total number of jumps per training session was 19.

For various strength exercises using body weight (also in conjunction with additional load), the volume refers to (a) the number of all repetitions of each exercise (for example, 20 chin-ups); (b) the sum of all repetitions per set or number of sets (for example, 3 x 10 push-ups); and (c) the sum total of all repetitions during a workout (for example, 200 repetitions using 10 different exercises within one circuit training).

For weightlifting exercises using the barbell, the volume is calculated on the basis of (a) the sum total of all weight lifted per training session (for example, 8 tons using 6 exercises); and (b) the number of repetitions performed with a given load (for example, 6 x 80 kg, or 3 x 6 x 80 kg).

2.2.4   The Stimulus Duration of Exercise

The stimulus duration of exercise refers to the time during which the physical exercise acts on the organism as a training stimulus. The weight stimulus, for example, can be very short but of great intensity, thus requiring relatively longer rest and admitting fewer repetitions; it can also be very long, thus acting as a sustained and uninterrupted stimulus culminating in complete exhaustion. The weight stimulus may also exert slight or medium stimulation intensity, allowing a relatively greater number of repetitions with relatively short rest periods.

The stimulus duration of exercise in cyclic activities represent the exercise time in seconds, minutes, or hours for a single loading (for example, 40 min of continuous endurance runs), or the sum total of all running times performed in all sets and/or series (for example, 3 x 3 min speed running generates 9 minutes of stimulus duration) within the total training session.

In acyclic activities the stimulus duration represents the time duration of a single loading, the effective exercise time for several repetitions within one set and/or the total duration of the training session in seconds and minutes.

The following relationships between the stimulus duration and stimulus intensity should be considered as a function of the nature of exercise:

- In cyclic activities the stimulus duration becomes shorter with increasing stimulus intensity at constant stimulus volume, as for example, when a runner runs a particular distance in a shorter time, i.e., covering it at a higher speed; or when a certain acyclic exercise with an equal number of repetitions, through a cyclic loading character during fitness training (standard loading), is mastered in an even shorter time, so that there is an increase in the strength applied per unit of time.

- In acyclic activities (for example, training with the barbell), an increase in the stimulus strength produces, by raising the external resistance (for example, increasing the weight of the barbell), a lengthening of the stimulus duration. The resulting lengthening of the tension stimulus acting upon the musculature is the main factor in the development of maximal strength.

It must, however, be noted that an increase in the stimulus density by way of shortening the recovery period without any essential modification of stimulus strength, volume, and duration of exercise produces only negligible development of maximal strength. Under these circumstances, the training effect can be seen more as a development of muscular endurance and the ability to resist fatigue. To improve maximal strength further, attempts should be made, above all, to increase the stimulus strength progressively by assuming a greater additional load while keeping the stimulus density and volume constant.

2.2.5   The Relationship between Intensity
and Volume of Exercise

In this section several diagrams are used to demonstrate the impor-

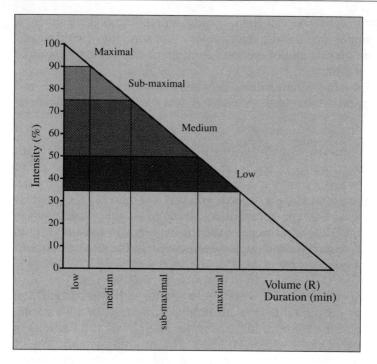

Figure 6   Diagram showing the relationship between intensity and
volume of exercise.

tance of the stimulus strength of an exercise within the context of
intensity of training. The exercise intensity is the deciding factor with
regard to stimulus levels or muscles, the nervous system, and other
organs. In other words, the intensity of exercise has a decisive effect
on an intensive functioning of all organs and systems involved during
every exercise. Intensity (work performed per unit of time) and volume (repetitions, exercise duration) of exercise are directly related to
each other, thus determining the level of exertion. The greater the
amount of work performed per unit of time, the sooner the fatigue levels are reached at which a continuation of the work becomes impossible. Thus, for example, a strong cyclist who is able to perform work of
1,200 kgm/min over a number of hours, can continue to perform work
of 1,800 kgm/min for an hour only and work of 2,400 kgm/min for a
few seconds only. A sprinter running at a speed of 15-18 km/h can

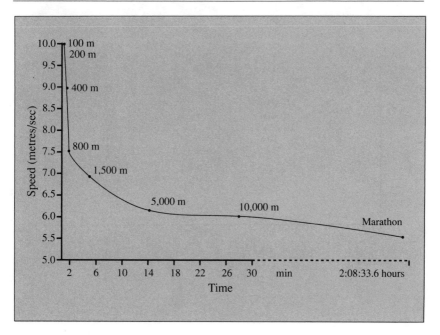

Figure 7   Diagram showing the relationship between distance and speed of running.

keep up this speed for 1-2 hours, but at a speed of 30 km/h can run for 0.5 minutes only. An athlete can achieve a performance of approximately 110 kgm/sec but is unable to sustain such performance beyond a few seconds.

The more the stimulus strength of exercise effects the body by high amounts of work performed per unit of time, the sooner physical work or exercise must be stopped on account of rapid fatigue build-up. Hence it is never possible to combine a maximal or very high application of strength with a large volume of exercise. Figure 6 represents the dependent relationship between intensity and volume of stimulus or exercise. Where the intensity of the applied strength, or the stimulus strength, is maximal, amounting to 90-100% of the maximal performance ability, the volume related to speed and time can only be small. And conversely, low intensity exercise can be sustained for a long period of time.

Similar relationships are shown in Figures 7 and 8. Figure 7

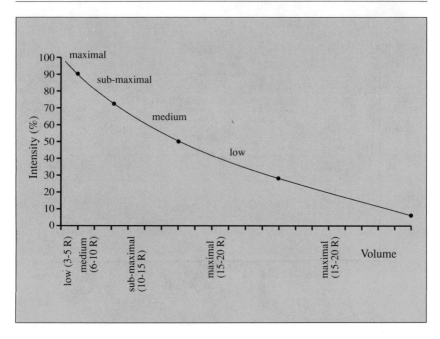

Figure 8   The relationship between intensity and volume of training
during strength workout using barbell (R-repetition).

demonstrates the relationship between speed and distance of running.
The running speed or the intensity of running decreases with increased
distance. In Figure 8, the relationship between resistance in weightlifting with a barbell and number of repetitions per set or volume of exercising is illustrated. Training at maximum or close to maximal resistance can be achieved only with a small number of repetitions and
long rest intervals between lifts. Conversely, during modest resistance
at 40-50% of maximal performance capacity, numerous repetitions per
set (20-30) are possible and require less rest between sets.

2.3   The Basic Training Methods

The components of training are closely interrelated and constantly
affect the athlete. The stimulus strength of exercise is of critical sig-
nificance. As a function of the stimulus intensity, the relationships

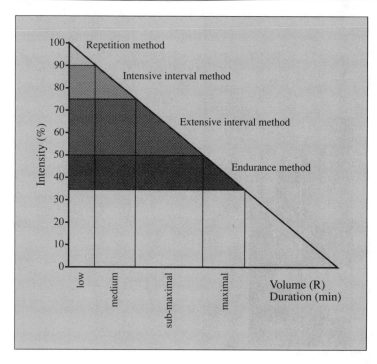

Figure 9   Basic training methods as a function of intensity and volume of exercise.

between stimulus density, volume, and duration tend to fluctuate. The stimulus strength within a chosen relative intensity range permits only a clearly defined and demarcated margin for the stimulus volume. Maximal stimulus strength necessitates minimal stimulus volume and vice versa. This, however, does not exclude a progressive increase in load, either through an increase in the stimulus strength at constant stimulus volume or through an increase the stimulus strength while retaining a constant stimulus intensity, provided that there is evidence of improvement in general and/or the sport-specific fitness. It is possible, too, to make simultaneous progressive modifications regarding the stimulus strength and volume, that is, within the limits of a particular range, depending on the direction of development of the athlete's fitness. Depending on the training goal, a progressive increase in load can also be achieved by modifying the stimulus density (by shortening

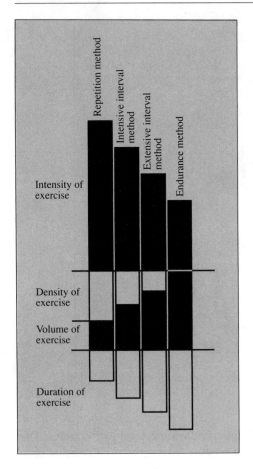

Figure 10   Basic training methods as a function of components of
               training.

the recovery period or by eliminating it altogether) and the structure
of the recovery period.

The interaction among the components of training is reflected in
the various loading methods, which characteristically use different
ranges of relative intensity. The transitions between these ranges of
intensity are fluid and are reflected in the four basic training methods:
endurance method, extensive interval method, intensive interval
method, and repetition method (26). These training methods are sum-

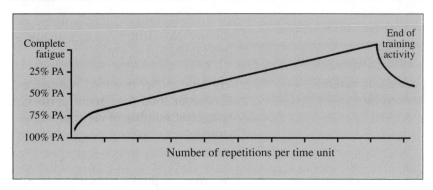

Figure 11   The accumulation of fatigue during the endurance method
              (PA -Athlete's performance ability).

marized below and also in Table 27, p. 114. The accompanying illustrations, Figures 9 to 14, further highlight the nature and the metho-
logical principles underlying the four trainings methods.

2.3.1   Endurance Method

Stimulus intensity
of exercise

• *Running:* training at 40-60% of maximal performance ability over a long
  distance; or training at 95-70% of
  maximal performance ability in competition or test runs over various distances (5, 10, 15, 20, 40 km).

• *Strength training:* working at approximately 50% of maximal performance
  ability using barbell exercises; or
  training at approximately 25-75% of
  the maximal repetition potential during general strength exercises.

Stimulus density
of exercise

• Exercising without a break.

Stimulus volume
of exercise

• *Running:* covering long distances (in
  km) per training unit or phase.

- *Strength training:* large volume of total weights lifted (in kg), using a large number of repetitions.

Stimulus duration
of exercise

- Very long (either one long continuous exercise or total time spent performing a great number of short exercises is long).

Physiological effect

- Cardiovascular efficiency, capillarization, oxygen intake capacity, aerobic capacity.

Training effect

- *Running:* basic endurance/long-term endurance.

- *Strength:* general endurance ability, muscular endurance ability.

Educational
and psychological effect

- Development of staying power, determination, self-confidence, psychophysical ability to mobilize oneself for hard work, ability to resist fatigue.

2.3.2   Extensive Interval Method

Stimulus intensity
of exercise

- *Running:* training at 60-80% of maximal performance ability.

- *Strength training:* working at 50-60% of maximal performance ability.

Stimulus density
of exercise

- A great number of repetitions of the exercise with a recovery period of approximately 30-90 seconds.

Stimulus volume
of exercise

- Each exercise (running or strength exercises) is repeated 20-30 times (also possible in sets).

Stimulus duration of exercise	• *Running:* depending on the distance. • *Strength training:* 15-30 seconds.
Physiological effect	• Cardiovascular efficiency, capillarization, oxygen intake capacity, aerobic capacity, buffer capacity.
Training effect	• *Running:* basic endurance, endurance over short, middle, and long distance. • *Strength training:* muscular endurance ability, power endurance ability, general endurance ability.
Educational and psychological effect	• Psychological and physical ability to mobilize oneself to do hard work, ability to improve performance, willpower, ability to resist fatigue, determination, self-confidence.

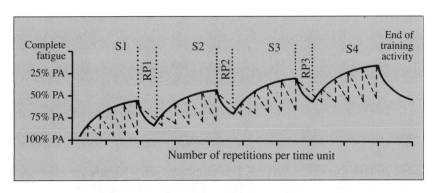

Figure 12   The accumulation of fatigue during the extensive interval method (S - Set; RP - Rest period between sets; PA - Athlete's performance ability).

2.3.3   Intensive Interval Method

Stimulus intensity of exercise

- *Running:* training at 80-90% of the maximal performance ability.

- *Strength training:* working at approximately 75% of the maximal performance ability.

Stimulus density of exercise

- 90-180 sec break.

Stimulus volume of exercise

- *Running:* approximately 10-12 repetitions.

- *Strength training:* 8-12 repetitions per set.

Stimulus duration of exercise

- *Running:* depending on the distance.

- *Strength training:* 8-15 sec.

Physiological effect

- Cardiovascular efficiency, capillarization, buffer capacity, energy potential, muscle cross-section, sensory-motor co-ordination, anaerobic capacity.

Training effect

- *Running:* speed, sprinting speed, short-term and medium-term endurance ability.

- *Strength training:* power and maximal strength, power endurance and muscular ability.

Educational and psychological effect

- Development of will-power, psychological and physical ability to mobilize oneself to work hard, ability to increase performance, ability to resist fatigue.

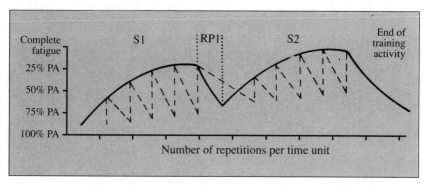

Figure 13   The accumulation of fatigue during the intensive interval
method (S - Set; RP - Rest period between sets; PA -
Athlete's performance ability).

During exercising using the extensive and intensive interval methods, the pulse rate typically reaches values of approximately 180 to 200 beats/min. After an incomplete recovery of some 45 to 180 seconds, the pulse will have dropped approximately to 120 to 140 beats/min.

2.3.3   Repetition Method

Stimulus strength *of exercise*	• *Running:* training at 90-100% of maximal performance ability. • *Strength training:* training at 80-95% (occasionally 100%) of maximal performance ability.
Stimulus density *of exercise*	• *Running:* recovery (depending on the distance) of approximately 3-45 min. • *Strength training:* 3-5 min.
Stimulus magnitude *of exercise*	• *Running:* 1-3 runs. • *Strength training*, depending on the stimulus strength: 1-3 or 3-6 repeti-

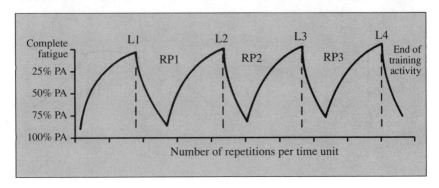

Figure 14   The accumulation of fatigue during the repetition method
(L - Load; RP - Recovery period; PA -Athlete's performance ability).

tions per set, or 20-30 individual repetitions.

Stimulus duration
of exercise

• *Running:* training essentially at a high
speed, depending on the distance: 3-8
sec, up to 15 sec, 20-60 sec, 2-10 min
up to approximately 30 min.

• *Strength training:* brief: the higher the
resistance to be overcome, the longer
the stimulus duration.

Physiological effect

• Energy potential, buffer capacity,
anaerobic capacity.

Training effect

• *Running:* loco-motor speed ability,
acceleration ability, jumping speed,
short- and medium-distance running
speed and, to some extent, long-term
endurance ability.

• *Strength training:* maximal strength
and power, power endurance and muscular endurance ability.

*Educational
and psychological effect*

• Development of will-power, psycho-physical ability to mobilize oneself for working at high speeds and for overcoming great resistance, mental and physical toughness, ability to improve performance, self-confidence.

3 Circuit Training: Methodology and Principles

3.1 Introduction

Circuit training (and its variations) is a method of fitness training that is designed to develop general, all-round physical and cardiovascular fitness. It is a training program that embraces a number of carefully selected exercises designed simultaneously to exercise in one session the four major muscle groups: legs, abdomen, arms and shoulders, and back and trunk. This aspect of circuit training is illustrated by the circuit training logo shown in Figure 15.

The loading of the main muscle groups changes as the athlete moves from one exercise to another. In a typical circuit training program each muscle group may be successfully loaded or exercised by several different exercises. The number of exercises per muscle group depends on (1) the training effect to be achieved; (2) the desired volume of work to be completed during a training session; (3) the desired intensity of effort; and (4) the structure of the program.

Each exercise within the circuit is numbered and is referred to as a station. The performer progresses from one exercise station to another in sequence, completing a prescribed amount of work (repetitions) at each exercise station. All the exercises designed to load one major muscle group are completed first before the performer moves on to the next station in the circuit.

The loading of the main muscle groups changes as the performer moves from one station to another. While one main muscle group is subjected to exercising, others are actively recovering. This aspect of circuit training, coupled with the fact that the performer does a prescribed number of repetitions at each station that is well below the maximum, allows the performer to move quickly from one station to

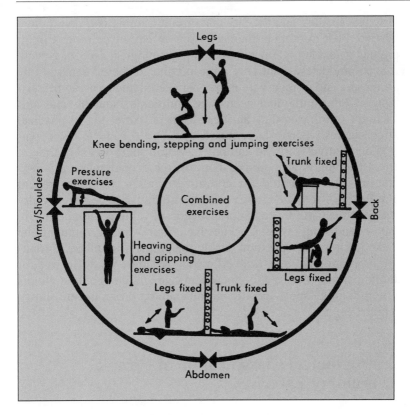

Figure 15   Circuit training logo.

another, requiring relatively little rest between exercising.

The entire circuit is usually repeated several times. Most school circuit training programs require that the single circuit be repeated about three times. In sports training the single circuit may be repeated up to six times. As the athlete briskly progresses from exercise to exercise fatigue starts to build up, and exercising on each subsequent lap becomes progressively more demanding, thus bringing about a strong positive training effect related to overall muscular strength and endurance. As the athlete requires little or no rest between exercises, the performer's heart rate remains relatively high throughout the circuit. This has a strong positive training effect on cardiovascular fitness.

Individual loading and the fact that circuit training is time efficient are the two most important characteristics of circuit training. Circuit training has valuable organizational and psychological aspects as well. It can accommodate a relatively large number of participants at one time; it requires no or relatively inexpensive equipment; it can be easily adapted to the individual needs and abilities of students and athletes. Circuit training is thus an ideal form of exercising in physical education classes where a large number of students has to be accommodated on relatively limited equipment within short period of time.

Circuit training is well suited, then, for the development of a general state of fitness in students and athletes alike. However, recent research has shown that a circuit training program can be successfully modified to meet the more specific needs of athletes competing in most sports and at all levels. Coaches have found circuit training to be an excellent form of preparation during the preparatory phase of training. Furthermore, due to its time efficiency it can be very effective for maintaining fitness during the precompetitive and competitive phases of training. Sample sport-specific circuit training programs are shown in Chapter 14.

3.2   Anatomical Classification of Circuit Training Exercises

Circuit training exercises ensure the development of an athlete's musculature system. They are thus classified on an anatomical basis to include the muscles of the legs, arms and shoulders, abdomen, and the back.

3.2.1   Exercises to Strengthen the Leg Musculature

This group of exercises includes all walking, running, hopping, jumping and stepping exercises, in which the foot, knee, and hip joints are made to bend and stretch and which contribute to a strengthening of the muscles of the feet, lower legs, thighs, and buttocks. Almost all exercises for developing the leg muscles also involve, to a certain degree, the iliopsoas, the abdominal, hip, and back muscles. In turn, the legs often participate in exercises designed to strengthen the back, arm, and shoulder muscles.

Exercises to develop the leg muscles are illustrated in Figures 1-46 on pages 136-140.

3.2.2 Exercises to Strengthen the Arm and Shoulder Musculature

Exercises intended for strengthening the arm, shoulder, and pectoral muscles, and to some degree, the back muscles, should be selected according to various criteria - such as whether the arms are to be used in bending or stretching movements, i.e., elbow flexion or extension for overcoming a resistance (your own body or apparatus). We can therefore distinguish between heaving or pressing, snatching, or throwing exercises and stretching, supporting, and pushing exercises. Gripping or holding exercises should be used for strengthening the hand and finger muscles. However, the individual movements (e.g., cleaning and jerking the barbell) complement each other, enabling trainees to grip and hold, heave and snatch, stretch and push consecutively. These exercises benefit in particular the trapezius, the lateral serrates, the deltoid, biceps and triceps, the muscles of the forearms (long and short radius extensor, radius and the flexors of the hand), as well as the large pectoral muscles and, to some extent, the long back extensor and the straight abdominal muscles.

Certain exercises for strengthening the arm and shoulder muscles put a great deal of strain on the lumbar region of the spine. Choose suitable positions to avoid injuries, i.e., seated or in riding posture with back support in a supine or prone position, as in Figures 67, 69, 92-95, pages 143, 144, and 146.

Exercises that develop the arm and shoulder musculature are shown in Figures 47-96 on pages 140-146.

3.2.3 Exercises to Strengthen the Abdominal Musculature

Exercises for the abdominal muscles all involve either a fixed trunk, with the legs stretched or curled up to the trunk or to the head; or fixed feet, with the trunk moving gradually to the thighs. In either case, the iliopsoas will have a significant part in these exercises. The abdominal muscles are also particularly strengthened by numerous barbell exercises, e.g., barbell swings with straight arms starting from the thighs up to a horizontal level, or above the head. These exercises are beneficial for the otherwise static abdominal muscles.

The exercises designed to develop the abdominal musculature are illustrated in Figures 97-120 on pages 146-149.

3.2.4   Exercises to Strengthen the Back Musculature

The back muscles are strengthened by all exercises including lifting motion or holding a load or the athlete's own trunk, arm, or leg weight. The back muscles are best exercised by raising the trunk from a forward-bent position into a hollow-back position with fixed legs (see Figure 130, p. 152) or by raising the legs with fixed trunk (e.g., inverted stretch hang at the wall bars, raising and lowering of the legs (see Figure 135, p. 153). The exercises should be done in such a way as to avoid injuries to the lumbar region of the spine. When in a bent position at an angle of approximately 90°, such as in Figure 129 a, p. 152, care must be taken to ensure that the main load does not rest upon the spine only, but that the lift is supported by simultaneous straightening of the legs. Furthermore, when doing barbell exercises injuries can be avoided by using the correct lifting technique. For example, the starting position for exercises illustrated in Figures 129 and 130, p. 152 requires a straight back with legs bent.

The exercises to develop the back musculature are shown in Figures 123-140 on pages 150-154.

3.2.5   Selecting the Exercises According
to Their Stimulus Strength

The development and improvement of the fitness-related abilities, strength, speed, and endurance in athletes depend mainly on the intensity of effort and on the stimulus strength of the exercises. The degree of exertion to be applied in selected exercises for general and specific fitness training should enable every athlete, depending on his or her abilities, to complete at least 10, and up to a maximum of 40, repetitions within any given set of exercises or at any given station. It should be noted, however, that if an exercise can be repeated more that 30 to 40 times per set, its effectiveness for the development of strength is significantly decreased. Only the cardiovascular fitness or aerobic endurance may benefit from using over 40 repetitions; the muscles will not become any stronger.

Experience has shown that developing strength requires up to 10 repetitions per exercise (the degree of exertion of the exercise and/or resistance permits up to 10 repetitions), whereas developing muscular endurance requires more than 10 but less than 30 repetitions per exercise (the degree of exertion of the exercise and/or resistance permits more than 10 but less than 30 repetitions). Therefore, depending on whether the aim of the training program is general or specific, and bearing in mind the intensity or resistance of effort required for each exercise, the repetitions at individual stations should be:

• for power development: 4-8 repetitions;
• for power-endurance development: 8-12 repetitions;
• for muscular endurance development: 14-25 repetitions;
• for endurance development: 30-40 repetitions.

Furthermore, the desired training effect also depends on other factors, such as: (1) the selection of the exercises; (2) the structure of the exercises within the training program; (3) the aim (developing general or specific fitness); (4) the degree of intensity and the degree of difficulty of the exercises; and, above all, (5) the selected loading method.

Depending on the chosen training method, the same exercise, such as bench press, may be effectively used to develop all components of strength (power, power endurance, muscular endurance). It is therefore not advisable to classify the exercises according to the intended training effect, but rather according to their specific character, such as:

• Exercises with a structure, identical, similar or dissimilar to that of competition exercises.
• Strength exercises for developing general or specific fitness.
• Flexibility exercises.
• Limbering and relaxation exercises.

For stronger athletes and students it is advisable to have additional loads on hand, such as medicine balls, sandbags, dumbbells, barbells, and so on. The exercises can then be performed with additional loadings and the degree of exertion can be varied. These combinations guarantee a multifaceted development of an athlete's strength.

3.3   Layout of Exercises Within a Circuit Training Program

Once they have been selected, the exercises need to be grouped according to the circuit training logo to insure an alternate loading of the four main muscular groups (Figure 15). It makes no difference as to how one views the diagram here. Depending on the training effect to be achieved, two or three different exercises done consecutively may be selected to act upon the same group of muscles. In general, it is a good idea to begin by exercising either the legs or the entire body. This enables the body's circulation to be well integrated right from the beginning of exercising. Although this consideration is of no importance for circuit training when applied to large groups, e.g., 30-40 stu-

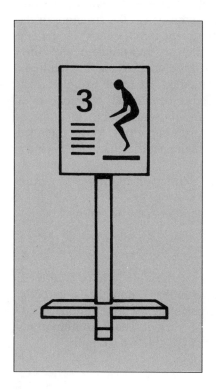

Figure 16   Sample circuit training stand.

dents or athletes, it does highlight the necessity of always commencing the circuit training program with a short but thorough warm-up in order to adequately prepare the cardiorespiratory system for rigorous circuit training exercising.

3.4   Designing Exercise Stations

It is important that the individual stations of a circuit are marked by well designed signs displaying the number of the station, a brief description of the exercise, a figure drawing of the exercise for orientation purposes, as well as the number of repetitions required for each exercise. The signs should be relatively large, and can be fixed to a wall or to a small stand, as shown in Figure 16. Initially it is also advisable to write the station number on the floor (Figure 17) and to use arrows to indicate the direction of the next station. The sequence of the stations should more or less form a circle, rectangle, or square, in order to make it easy for large-sized classes or training groups to find the next station. The numbers on the floor and the signs should be immediately visible when changing stations. The value of a circuit training program will be greatly diminished if it does not conform to this structure.

3.5   Introducing Circuit Training Program to Students and Athletes

Students and athletes should be introduced to a circuit training program in a highly organized manner. To generate the necessary motivation in students, the teacher or coach must explain the objectives and potential benefits of the program, as well as outline its structure and procedures. Prepared performance cards (see Table 1) should then be distributed to each performer. To acquaint the pupils or athletes with the exercises, the teacher or coach (and well-coordinated, more experienced students or athletes who can be used as demonstrators) should demonstrate the execution of each exercise by walking the group through the program, moving from station to station, slowly and systematically, to ensure (1) the correct execution of each exercise; (2) the understanding of the proper sequence of exercising; and (3) the

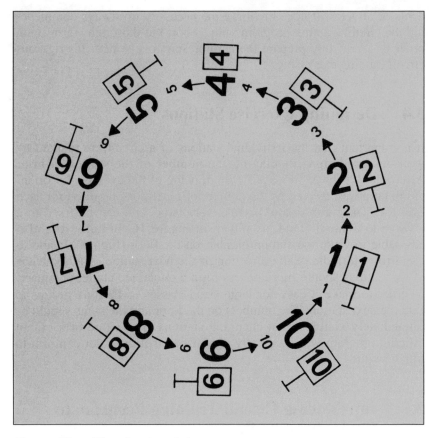

Figure 17   The circuit training sequence.

correct method of recording the results on on the individual performance cards.

It is a good practice for the teacher to test the exercises for feasibil-
ity and degree of loading beforehand, on a number of reliable pupils.
Indeed, it is an essential prerequisite for the successful application of
circuit training. Remember: where possible, no more than three pupils
should be allotted to one station.

The students may then become better acquainted with these exercises by trying them out themselves. After this preliminary trial, one
student should be selected to demonstrate the exercises again at each

Table 1   Sample performance record card.

Name:	Age: Height:: Weight::					
Exercise	RM Test 1 Date	$\dfrac{RM}{2} \times 1$ Date	$\dfrac{RM}{2} \times 2$ Date	$\dfrac{RM}{2} \times 3$ Date	RM Test 2 Date	$\dfrac{RM}{2} \times 1$ Date
1						
2						
3						
4						
5						
6						
7						
8						
9						
10						
No. of Reps.						
Exer. Time						
Pulse (HR/10 sec)	1 2 3 4	1 2 3 4	1 2 3 4	1 2 3 4	1 2 3 4	1 2 3 4

RM   = Repetition Maximum
Pulse = 1 - before exercise; 2- immediately after exercise; 3 -1 min after exercise; 4 - 2 min after exercise.

station. At that stage, any faults of execution can be corrected by the teacher. It is important to stress the accurate execution of the exercises at all times, but particularly for the *maximum performance score test* designed to establish individual circuit training loads. Without this direction, students will tend to attempt as many repetitions as possible at the expense of good execution.

The students must also be instructed how correctly to count the number of repetitions they perform at each exercise station. It has been observed in almost all test groups that pupils and athletes get their counts wrong if they have not been closely briefed.

Establishing height and distance check-marks is desirable for specific exercises such as jumps, medicine-ball throws and pushes, etc. Otherwise it is not possible to make comparisons in work performed between individual athletes. Where the training goal is set primarily to improve power by means of intensive and explosive strength application, 6-10 repetitions without any time limit is recommended.

The teacher may allocate a "start number" to the performance record card of each pupil, indicating at which station he or she is to start. Alternatively, the pupils can enter the sequence of stations on their cards during the first test lap. For instance, a pupil starting at station 6, enters a 6 on the performance record card under the column marked "exercises." Thereafter, for each lesson in which circuit training he or she carries out, the sequence 6, 7, 8, 9, 10, 1, 2, 3, 4, 5 will be compulsory. If this sequence is not strictly adhered to, a noticeable improvement in performance at the individual stations can no longer be assured because the number of repetitions will become unbalanced. If, for example, a student has to do chin-ups at station 1 and climb the pole at station 10, the individual performance quota will not be achieved if the order of the circuit is changed.

3.6   The First Maximum Performance Score Test

To correctly establish the amount or load of individual training each performer can accommodate, maximum performance score tests are used on a regular basis. To avoid extreme muscle soreness or injuries the first test should take place only after the students become gradually accustomed to circuit training. This is accomplished by performing each of the exercises that comprise the circuit at a slower rate and with a reduced load, placing little or no emphasis on time. Again, the form of the execution is of major concern here. After several sessions, normally 3-5, students should be ready to perform their First

Maximum Performance Score Test to establish the bench mark, their first repetition maximum (RM), at each exercise station. For successful testing follow these steps:

• All students or athletes should take up the starting position at their respective stations and wait for the signal to begin.

• All athletes begin their exercises at the same time at a whistle or command. The exercising time will be restricted to 30 seconds. Again, a whistle ends the exercising.

• In physical education programs in schools this is followed by a 30-second break. During each break the pupils enter the number of repetitions achieved on their performance record cards, then change to the next station and take up the starting position.

• Upon the agreed command they all start exercising again at the same time.

If the first maximum performance score test is conducted in this way, 10 minutes' exercising time will be required for 10 exercises. Since it is possible to lose track of the sequence when there are so many simultaneous exercises, the teacher or coach should appoint one student at the beginning of the circuit to announce when the 10th station is reached. In this way, the teacher is better able to concentrate on the stop watch and general flow of action in the gym. The use of a tape recorder for giving commands is an excellent way of freeing the teacher from this demanding task. The use of popular music between commands should further stimulate the students' enthusiasm for the exercises.

Teaching students and athletes how to take and record their pulse before and after the circuit is an important aspect of circuit training. Regular pulse measurements may be effectively used to assess the processes by which the cardiovascular system adapts to training from week to week. A continuous fall in the pulse rate after exercising over several weeks indicates an improvement in cardiovascular fitness. The teacher or coach must decide whether the pulse rate is to be measured after the maximum performance score test only or after each circuit training session. As a rule, the pulse rate should be measured over 10-second measuring periods, four times: prior to and immediately after circuit, and also 1 and 2 minutes after exercising has stopped.

It is advisable to practise pulse rate measurement during health or gym classes well before circuit training is introduced. Initially, it should be explained that the pulse-beat can be located at the carotid artery by using the thumb or index or forefinger. (Some pupils may need to be helped finding the carotid pulse.) Once this technique is mastered, the pupils will proceed to count their pulse rates over a period of 10 seconds. Errors in calculation can best be avoided by entering the values measured over 10 sec onto the performance record card.

The commands used for measuring pulse rates are: "Attention, pulse!". After a quick count "1, 2, 3 - Go!" the pulse is measured. "Stop" indicates the end of the 10 sec measuring period.

3.7   The Individual Training Load

The repetition maximum (RM) values achieved at each exercise station during the maximum performance score test are used as the bench mark for individual training load. The individual RM values, divided by 2 or 4, that is,

$$\frac{RM}{2} \quad or \quad \frac{RM}{4},$$

have proven their usefulness in physical education programs in schools and also as preparatory training for competition. For competitive training, it is recommended that the training load be expressed in percentages (for example, 50% or 70% of the maximal performance ability).

The initial training load, which must be fixed individually, is used until the subsequent maximum performance score test sets new standards. The improvement achieved in performance will then represent the initial value for the new training load. For example: if an athlete achieved 20 repetitions of a given exercise during the first maximum performance score test, the individual training load being RM/2=10 repetitions, and in the second maximum performance score test he or she accomplished 30 repetitions, the new training load should be fixed at RM/2=15 repetitions. This is the principle of progressive loading. With dumbbell exercises, for example, progressive loading can be achieved by increasing either the number of repetitions or the weight of the dumbbell, or else by reducing the lifting time but leaving the weight the same. The method used is dependent on the desired training effect.

3.8   The Educational Value of Circuit Training in Schools

Circuit training can make a valuable contribution to the physical education of the young. Its adoption in schools has produced a noticeable improvement in behaviour and discipline among students when they train together. Circuit training is characterized by a genuine and productive training atmosphere. None of the students becomes overloaded, for they exercise at each station according to an individually determined loading. The interest of the students in circuit training is encouraged when they are able to record the development of their own fitness and to observe individual and collective performance first hand. In practice, it has been observed that the pupils tend to lose interest when exercise programs remain unchanged over a long period, or the same training load is applied to all pupils, or individual performance is not recorded. Exercising then become monotonous and initial enthusiasm begins to wane. Recording fitness development encourages self-reliance and fosters integrity and individuality. Individually designed circuit training programs encourage even weaker performers to undertake strenous physical activity at a suitable loading, because they do not feel compelled to attempt more than they are capable of. The exercises at each station are simple enough to make each student feel a sense of achievement in completing them. This sense of achievement is also generated by the repetitive maximum performance score tests: each student is able to observe his progress from his performance record card and observe how his progress develops through mastering a higher number of repetitions over a given period of time or through exercising for a shorter period at a standard training load. This helps to enhance the self-confidence of students of a weaker physical constitution especially.

Circuit training is an excellent way of eliciting self-reliance and initiative in students. Students can be asked to prepare the exercise station themselves, for example. Thus, one pupil can be made responsible for putting up the signs for the individual stations, another can hand out the performance record cards and collect them at the end of the training session. Pupils themselves should be encouraged to erect the apparatus at the station where they begin their circuit, and dismantle it at the point where they finish. In this way, the assembling and dismantling of the stations requires no more than 2 minutes. It helps if the circuit is arranged in such a way that the apparatus does not have to be moved too far from its permanent location in the gymnasium.

Circuit training makes the pupils respect and appreciate each other's performance. The teacher or coach should impress on all pupils that the most important criterion is individual improvement in performance when a second maximum performance score test is conducted, approximately 4 weeks after the first. The teacher can point out that it will be much more difficult for a student to improve on a very good performance on the first maximal test than a weaker student to improve a lower score.

Classifying the circuits into different ability levels will help deepen the interest of students in the program. The teacher may initially suggest that all exercises be performed using the same degree of exertion. All pupils may initially be set to train on the easy or "white" circuit. Students who achieve a certain number of repetitions or laps are then allowed to move to the more demanding "red" circuit. Often, as a result, they become eager to do extra training at home so as to be able to perform circuit exercises at the next level all the sooner.

Awards in recognition of individual improvement in performance (such as a colored ribbon attached to the gym outfit) should help foster healthy competition. The performance of a weaker student should not go unacknowledged, especially if a more accomplished athlete has not shown much ambition or energy in training, and has thus suffered a setback in performance. Indeed, in the latter, the teacher may wish to exclude such a student from an award, even though in absolute terms it was a better performance. Teachers may also wish to post results - of each class on a notice board as well as arrange to have the best pupils from each class compete over one circuit lap.

3.9 Educational Principles and Basic Requirements of Circuit Training

The integrated educational and character-building value of a sports training session is based on the application and implementation of a number of general and specific training principles. These principles can be formulated as rules:

- "Exercise to promote your health!"
- "Vary your exercises!"
- "Select those exercises and methods which you are able to cope with!"
- "Do your exercises regularly and set yourself targets!"
- "Repeat your training program over a long period!"
- "Increase your training load systematically!"
- "Follow the correct pedagogical principles!"
- "Train regularly in order to keep your strength, speed, and endurance abilities stable, even over periods of forced inactivity!"
- "Train to suit your age, fitness and health!"

These principles are described below in greater detail.

3.9.1   Training to Promote Health

If the overall aim is to promote health, circuit training must be organized and implemented in accordance with the combined experience of coaches, teachers, physiologists, and sports physicians. Exercises for circuit training must be selected and arranged so as to ensure a significant change in the loading of the main muscle groups according to the circuit training logo. Teachers and coaches must therefore be thoroughly acquainted with musculature (location, insertion and origin) and with basic exercise physiology. They must also be able to assess the degree of difficulty of the individual exercises and the necessary intensity of the effort to be applied in these exercises in order to design an individualized and feasible training load at each exercise station. For instance, the periodicity of the exercises in circuit training (whether they extend over one, two, or three laps, with or without a break), depends on the nature of the training load (ratio between the number of repetitions and intensity of exercise). The teacher or coach is also expected to judge the impact a circuit training program by observing the performer's behaviour and other physiological signs (outbreak of sweating, muscle shivering, reddening or paleness, breathing; also see p. 18), especially the pulse readings. Pulse measurements prior to and immediately after a specified break are therefore indispensable. A reduced pulse rate after unchanged loading is, for instance, an obvious indication of a successful adaptation and a functionally higher level of fitness (3, 27, 34).

Finally, performers should learn how to assess themselves during and after training. A training stress scale based on individual emotional states and designed for self-assessment can be found in Table 2. Based on these loading characteristics, every athlete should be able to sense the extent or magnitude of experienced exertion and in turn of his or her total training load.

When training athletes, coaches should follow a fundamental rule: the fewer the number of weekly training sessions, the higher the degree of individual training loading. Daily training should involve, at the most, two to three loading peaks per week (possibly of stage 4 or 5 intensity level). When exercising during circuit training the loading should be estimated individually: between stages 2 and 3 for the first lap, between stages 3 and 5 for the second lap, and between stages 4 and 5 for the third lap. The individual training load can be increased either rapidly or gradually on the basis of self-assessment and on the basis of pulse rate values. This applies particularly to training for competition. It must be remembered that a training load which from an athlete's subjective point of view may be characterized by a loading equivalent to stages 1 and 2 only, cannot, in the long run, produce any training effect in the form of a substantial increase in any kind of performance.

3.9.2   Varying the Exercises

The program of exercises should be compiled so that the main muscular groups are subjected to several exercises of varying loadings; some of these should be combined exercises. Experience has shown that ten exercises can be compiled for one training program so as to release a variety of positive developmental stimuli. It is then possible to load each muscle group (arm, shoulder, abdominal, back, leg muscles) by two different exercises and to load the whole body by using two combined exercises. A program consisting of 8 to 12 different exercises should emphasize versatility. General circuit training programs may be complemented by other programs to suit specific sports. However, it is better to exclude exercises involving technical difficulties from programs for specific sports; only simple exercises or those that have been technically well mastered should be included.

Table 2:   A training stress scale designed to assess the degree of exertion during circuit training.

Stage 1 Active Recovery
Relaxed and enjoyable exercising which produces optimal psycho-physical compensation (that is, an optimal physical and mental recovery) and normal-to-very-good appetite and sleep.

Stage 2 Low Loading
Easy training, partly "playful," training load hardly noticeable (i.e., low demands on the cardiovascular system and the nervous-musclular apparatus), physical and mental well-being after training; normal-to-very-good appetite and sleep.

Stage 3 Medium Loading
Training with slightly noticeable load (medium demands on the cardiovascular system and the nervous-muscular apparatus); a slight sense of fatigue after training; normal-to-very-good appetite and sleep.

Stage 4 Sub-maximal Loading
Training with appreciable loading stimuli (i.e., sub-maximal demands on the cardiovascular system and nervous-muscular apparatus); slight fatigue during training, increased need for rest and sleep after training; appetite and sleep are normal to very good.

Stage 5 Maximal Loading
Training with very appreciable loading stimuli (i.e., very high demands on the cardiovascular system and nervous-muscular apparatus), symptoms of fatigue during training; appreciable need for rest and sleep, after which physical and mental freshness is regained.

Stage 6 Overexertion
Training with performance demands requiring extreme determination; very high fatigue after training (possibly symptoms of exhaustion); excessive desire for rest and sleep, followed by residual fatigue; little, if any, appetite; poor and restless sleep in spite of great desire for sleep.

Varied loading of the individual muscular groups through different exercises accords with the principles of health education. But, the principle of variety also has its limits and must be subjected to a specific purpose in training. There are varying limits on versatility, depending on whether an athlete is engaged in basic, intermediate, or highly competitive training. The next principle is derived directly from these considerations.

3.9.3   Selection of Exercises and Training Methods to Suit Individual Needs

This principle is of prime importance, especially in the choice of training method for circuit training. These methods are described in detail in chapters 4 to 7. The essence of each training method is characterized by the interplay between the various training factors: stimulus intensity, stimulus density, volume, and duration of the stimulus (see Figures 9 to 14, Chapter 2). The underlying characteristics of the methods (endurance, extensive and intensive interval method, repetition method) are based on the physiological laws that govern the development and improvement of the fitness-related abilities, strength, speed, and endurance.

Application of the relevant rules in circuit training requires familiarity with means and methods beforehand, especially in training for competition, when the maintenance of a general or specific ability and compensation for high loadings for specific sports are essential. Hence, depending on the objective of circuit training and the particular sport, only modifications of circuit training that develop or maintain basic fitness should be incorporated into programs. A middle-distance runner must therefore not be subjected to circuit training based on the repetition method, which applies to throwers, shot-putters and jumpers. Circuit training based on the endurance method or the extensive interval method are, however, particularly suited to runners.

Physical education programs in schools should consist mainly of circuit-training programs using general development exercises and only in special cases should the specific circuit training programs be used. Initially the exercises chosen should not involve any additional loading to the performer's own body weight, or if they do, the loading should represent only standard resistances (medicine balls, horizontal bar, dumbbells, sandbags, partners). Exercises with additional loading in the form of variable resistances (e.g., barbell) may be assigned to young athletes over the age of 14 only if the weight of the barbell does not represent more than a third or approximately half the athlete's body weight. Even so, circuit training based on the repetition method is not applicable to school programs.

Circuit training should not involve complicated technical elements. It must, however, not be assumed from this that circuit training programs must be completely devoid of specifically developing exercises. Such exercises may, indeed, be included in circuit training provided that their execution technique is properly mastered by young athletes.

Finally, the designed circuit training program must meet the desired training objectives of the athlete. In an attempt, for example, to develop general endurance one should not design a circuit training program based on the repetition method. Similarly, to develop maximal strength one should not apply circuit training based on the endurance method. The effectiveness of circuit training program can be examined by a number of tests. These tests are outlined below.

Proposed Physical Fitness Tests

Although regular maximum performance score tests permit a fair indication of the dynamics of individual fitness of an athlete at any time, it is nevertheless advisable to carry out simple tests to determine the complex development of physical fitness in a student or athlete. The tests prescribed for the physical fitness badge in Germany are suitable requirements as are the tests approved by German physical education instructor and coaches:

• *Maximal Strength Tests*
Sports Training:
Weight exercises such as clean and jerk (classic style) using squat or split technique, bench press, squats with barbell behind neck, leg extension strength test on the leg bench at different knee angles.

Maximal strength tests are not recommended for school programs.

• *Explosive Power Tests*
Sports training and school programs:
Squats with barbell (10 repetitions, time recorded), star jumps (height

essential, number of jumps unimportant), triple and quintuple hopping on right and left leg, standing triple jump, standing long jump, standing high jump, high jump from squat position, shot-putting from standing position, shot-throwing forward, backward.

• *Power Endurance Tests*
Sports training and school programs:
Running over 100 m from crouch start, running over 150 m, 300 m and 400 m distance, 2-minute run (distance measured in m), squat thrusts and stretch jumps (time and number recorded), Japan test, bicycle ergometer test.

• *Speed Tests*
Sports training and school programs:
30-m run with flying start, 30-m run from standing position, 60-m run from standing position or crouch start, hopping jumps over 30 m (time and number of jumps recorded), or 10 jumps on one leg (time and distance recorded).

• *Muscular Endurance Tests*
Sports training and school programs:
Rope climbing by using hands only (time and number recorded), squat thrusts and stretch jumps (time and number recorded), push-ups (number recorded), chin-ups (number recorded), bicycle ergometer test, hand crank ergometer test, Japan test (time recorded).

• *Endurance Tests*
Sports training and school programs:
Graded endurance running test (3 x 5 min up to 3 x 10 min: 1st grade or low speed, 2nd grade or medium speed, 3rd grade or high speed) bicycle ergometer test, Harvard step test; swimming over 100 m, 400 m or 10,000 m distance, or swimming from 5 to 40 min (distance recorded).

3.9.4   Regular Training With an Objective

The educational potential of circuit training becomes fully effective only if its objectives are met. Teachers and coaches must proceed with caution when introducing circuit training. They need to describe to their trainees the fitness abilities that are to be developed by circuit training, the loading method to be selected, the discipline, cooperation, self-reliance, and confidence necessary to perform the exercises. Teachers who are enthusiastic about the program will transmit that enthusiasm and conscientiousness to their pupils. The enthusiasm of students should itself engender success, which in turn will produce a strong desire to improve performance, especially since they are responsible for monitoring it themselves. For that reason the issue of evaluation of the performance (see Chapter 11, pp. 189-102) that have been achieved in circuit training gains special importance in school programs. The issue of education is of lesser important for athletes who are training for competitive performance. They are expected, as a rule, to have a conscientious attitude towards training. They too, however, need the feeling of success, inner satisfaction, and self-confidence that comes from success at control tests, informal competitions and, of course, maximum performance score tests.

3.9.5   Repeating the Training Program over a Long Period

Repetition allows the improvement of an athlete's general and specific performance. Without it, a trainee's body is not provoked sufficiently to move to a higher level of fitness. It follows, then, that once a circuit training program has proved successful, it should be retained over a longer period. Although this requirement applies particularly to sports training (for all training stages: basic, build-up, and competitive training), it is also relevant to physical education programs in schools. As a rule, a circuit training program should not be changed until it has been performed over a period of at least 4-6 weeks. Proof of adaptation rarely becomes evident before such a period, although an improvement in performance may be apparent as early as 3 weeks after regular training. Circuit training, then, should be practised regularly and not sporadically. Conversely, stagnation in performance is often an indication that a standard program applied over a longer period has failed to produce further improvement in performance, which, at this stage, can now be achieved only through an increase of load or through an introduction of a new set of exercises.

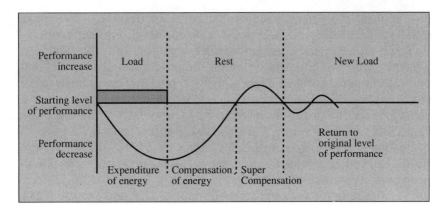

Figure 18   Changing phases of performance ability during exercise
                and recovery (12).

3.9.6   Increasing the Training Load Gradually and Systematically

Exercising systematically using circuit training requires a gradual and progressive increase of training load. Research and coaching experience have shown that the human organism can adapt slowly and gradually to systematic increases in training load over time. It is therefore imperative in circuit training that the entire loading is gradually increased on the basis of maximum performance score tests carried out on a regular basis. The results achieved on these tests form the basis for the new training load, which is determined individually, and remains operative until the next test sets new standards.

It is important that the athlete or pupil not vary the order in which the exercises of the circuit are performed. To do so would make it difficult to measure accurately the onset of fatigue. In practice, this means that trainees must repeat the chosen sequence of exercises for the maximum performance score test and also for the individually prescribed training load. If they do not, it will be impossible to measure systematic improvement in performance at each exercising station.

Systematic training requires regular attendance and the formulation of a program which, when broken down into individual lessons over the course of weeks, months, and a year, guarantees a purposeful

Table 3 Regular application of circuit training during one physical education lesson/week. The exercise load systematically increases from week to week.

Week	Lesson	Exercise Load (Reps.)	No. of Laps	Exercising Time from ... to (min of the lesson)
1	1	RM Test 1		30 to 45
	2	—		—
2	1	$\dfrac{RM}{2}$	x 1	1 to 10 or 30 to 40
	2	—		—
3	1	$\dfrac{RM}{2}$	x 2	5 to 25 or 20 to 45
	2	—		—
4	1	$\dfrac{RM}{2}$	x 3	5 to 35
	2	—		—
5	1	RM Test 2		30 to 45

RM = Repetition Maximum

increase of training load in circuit training. Jakovlev (12) was the first to describe the dynamics of training load and rest period and the necessity of gradually increasing the training load over time. This is shown in Figures 18 and 19. These dynamics also govern the systematic application of circuit training for general and sport-specific fitness training. It is recommended that school programs also apply progressive increases in loading. A few examples below will demonstrate the systematic approach of designing circuit training for physical education classes. These examples depend on two 45-minute lessons a week (see Tables 3 to 5).

The examples demonstrate that systematic application of circuit

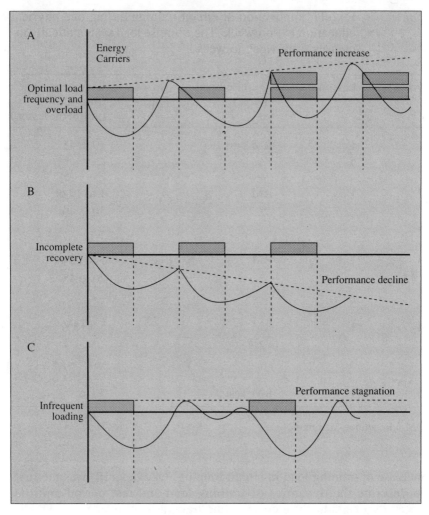

Figure 19   Performance as a function of loading dynamics. A - any
              training activity carried out showing the "Super compen-
              sation" phase with the loading level gradually increasing
              results in an increase in performance; B - repetition carries
              out during incomplete recovery results in a performance
              decline; C - if the repetition is carried out when the traces
              of previous loading have diminished, the performance
              level remains unchanged.

Table 4   Regular application of circuit training during two physical
             education lessons/week. The exercise load systematically
             increases from week to week.

Week	Lesson	Exercise Load (Reps.)	No. of Laps	Exercising Time from ... to (min of the lesson)
1	1	RM Test 1		30 to 45
	2	$\dfrac{RM}{2}$	x 1	1 to 10, or 30 to 40
2	1	$\dfrac{RM + 2}{2}$	x 2	5 to 25, or 20 to 45
	2	$\dfrac{RM + 3}{2}$	x 1	1 to 15, or 30 to 45
3	1	$\dfrac{RM + 1}{2}$	x 3	5 to 40
	2	$\dfrac{RM + 3}{2}$	x 1	1 to 15, or 30 to 45
4	1	RM Test 2		30 to 45
	2	$\dfrac{RM}{2}$	x 1	1 to 15, or 30 to 45

RM = Repetition Maximum

training combines a number of advantages: overloading can be avoided; there is no monotony; the interest of the pupils in exercising is kept alive because the individual improvement in performance can be closely monitored by the entries on the performance record cards. Each of these examples also shows that circuit training does not have to overwhelm sports lessons in schools; it can be effectively carried out at the beginning or end of each lesson, leaving enough time for other activities.

Table 5 Regular application of circuit training during one physical education lesson/week. The exercise load systematically increases from week to week by increasing the number of repetitions/set. The number of laps remains the same.

Week	Lesson	Exercise Load (Reps.)	No. of Laps	Exercising Time from ... to (min of the lesson)
1	1	RM Test 1		30 to 45
	2	—		—
2	1	$\dfrac{RM + 1}{2}$	x 2	5 to 25, or 20 to 45
	2	—		—
3	1	$\dfrac{RM + 2}{2}$	x 2	5 to 25, or 20 to 45
	2	—		—
4	1	$\dfrac{RM + 3}{2}$	x 2	5 to 25, or 20 to 45
	2	—		—
5	1	RM Test 2		30 to 45

RM = Repetition Maximum

It is also possible to use other structured approaches to develop physical potential of students, as is evident from these examples. Experience has shown that it is advisable to carry out maximal performance score tests always at the end of a physical education lesson. When only one lap is being used, for example, it makes no difference whether the circuit training is scheduled at the beginning or the end of the lesson. However, for organizational consistency, it is advisable to decide on one routine and to follow it throughout. The exercise time and load recommended in Tables 3 to 5 can be modified to suit existing requirements.

3.9.7 Follow the Main Pedagogical Principles

In compiling a circuit program one must also remember the following pedagogical principles:

- Proceed from simple to more complex.
- Proceed from easy to more challenging.
- Proceed from familiar to more unfamiliar.
- Proceed from general to more specific.

Proceeding from simple to more complex means including simple exercises requiring simple technique. Skilled movements and technical elements are recommended only when they are properly mastered by all participants. The younger the trainees, the simpler the exercises should be. This requires that all participants are familiar with the circuit program, its layout in the gym, and the individual exercising stations.

Proceeding from easy to more challenging implies that the loading level of every exercise must vary. This enables the teacher or coach to take into consideration the current fitness of the performer when allotting the individual training load. Individual loads can also be set by allowing athletes to perform an exercise in a different way or by adding weight. It is a useful teaching device to use colour to denote varying training levels of difficulty in circuit training.

When *proceeding from familiar to unfamiliar,* it is advisable to use only exercises that are well known to the performers when compiling a circuit training program. Care should be taken always to ensure that the pupils or athletes have sufficient time to acquaint themselves with the new exercises. It is important to know the starting and final positions of each exercise, as the number of repetitions achieved must be counted correctly.

Proceeding from general to more specific applies, above all, to the specific conditioning in competitive sports. The transition from the general to the specific fitness does not necessarily constitute a linear development; rather, it is an overlapping process. It is a basic teaching practice at the beginning of a new training season to bring the general athletic performance of an athlete up to the level previously achieved, or to bring it to a completely new and higher level. The methodical approach for general conditioning in training must be applied. Both the exercises and the methodology of exercising must also guarantee a direct development of the specific performance ability by the general conditioning. When the effect of general fitness conditioning stagnates exercises need to be changed, and the program restructured to include specific training methods that develop a performer's essential fitness-related abilities for competition. Again, once the effect of these programs has worn off, they too must be replaced with new ones. This process of developing specific performance has been described as the zig-zag effect (33).

3.9.8   Train Regularly to Keep the Fitness Abilities Stable

Circuit training will have realized its purpose only if the improvement of general and specific physical performance remains stable over a long period. A completely new and stable level of general and/or specific fitness cannot be maintained if training is restricted to a short period. Strength, speed, and endurance may be achieved relatively quickly by intensive training, but the resulting physiological adaptation processes of the organism can be lost as quickly as they have been gained, should training be discontinued (28).

It is necessary, then, to continue circuit training systematically over a longer training period. Circuit training is best suited to an indoor environment, such as a gymnasium, and the ideal time for its use is therefore from November to March. Remember: the stability of a high level of fitness is proportionally related to the length of time it was acquired. Vigorous application of circuit training over several winter months will stabilize an athlete's general and specific fitness even over periods of forced inactivity brought about by injuries and by other unforeseen circumstances.

3.9.9   Training to Suit Age, Fitness, and Health
of the Performer

Research and experience have shown that children and youth when subjected to equivalent loading stimuli per kilogram of body weight recover and adapt similarly to adults. However, according to Mellerowicz (17), the total training load resulting from the sum of loading factors (intensity, density, number, and duration of stimuli) must be significantly lower than in adults. It is therefore important always to bear in mind the age of the performer when designing circuit training. Together with the correct proportion between load and recovery, this ensures the training most appropriate to the age of the athlete. When training according to age, the teacher or coach must decide whether the individual load is to be calculated in percentage of the individual's RM or by the suggested formula

$$\frac{RM}{2}.$$

A correctly determined training load suitable to one's age will result in the achievement of an optimal training effect. Circuit training programs that continuously demand maximal loading, whether with or without time limit, should never be considered for school programs. With a high loading demand at individual exercising stations the initial rest period of approximately 30 sec must neither be shortened nor altogether eliminated for health reasons. Disregarding this principle means acting in a rather irresponsible manner and it may result in students refusing circuit training altogether.

4 Circuit Training Based on the Endurance Method

Circuit training by the endurance method requires exercising for up to three laps without a rest period between laps or exercises. Variations of this program include:

1. exercising without a rest period and without any target time for one or several laps;
2. exercising without a rest period and with a target time for three laps; and
3. exercising without a rest period for a specified time.

4.1 Variation 1

This method requires no rest period and no target time. After the athlete has learned the exercises and has been tested for the maximal number of repetitions using the maximum performance score test (see p. 65), he or she is given the following training load:

$$\frac{RM}{2} \quad \text{or} \quad \frac{3RM}{4}.$$

The athlete starts the exercises at the first station and moves in a previously arranged order from one station to the next, performing them at a relaxed pace. The teacher sets the number of laps. With ten stations the maximal number of laps in schools is three, in sports training it is up to six. Each athlete or student then enters the time achieved on a performance record card (for example, one lap=5 min, two laps=12:13 min, three laps=17:20 min).

Loading Alternatives

a. The individual number of exercises is increased, for instance, from

$$\frac{3\,RM}{4} \quad \text{to} \quad \frac{3\,RM+2}{4} \quad \text{to} \quad \frac{RM+3}{2}$$

and so on, while the exercise time for one to three laps remains the same.

b. The exercise time is shortened for one to three laps when the circuit routine remains the same.

c. The load level is increased by a adding a weight to the body weight exercises while the exercise time remains the same.

Ranges of Application for Variation 1

• Sports Training Program
(a) track and field (for sprinters, middle- and long-distance runners, and sometimes athletes doing several events); (b) all ball games; (c) swimming, cycling, boxing, judo, rowing, mountaineering, skiing (see circuit training programs for specific sports, p. 191).

• School Programs
12-plus age group. The standard load is

$$\frac{RM}{4}$$

using body weight exercises with or without additional weights. Each student keeps his own performance record card updated, as shown in Tables 6 and 7.

4.2   Variation 2

This method requires no rest and a target time for three laps. After all the exercises are mastered and after having taken the maximum performance score test (i.e., 30 sec of exercising and 30 sec of rest), the exercising time which the athlete is required to complete in one lap is tested by using the load of

$$\frac{3\,RM}{4} \quad \text{or} \quad \frac{RM}{2}.$$

Table 6   Sample performance record card for circuit training based on the endurance method. There is no rest period between sets and laps and there is no target time for completion.

Name: Age:
                                                   Height:
                                                   Weight:

Exercise	RM Test 1 Date	$\dfrac{RM}{2}$ x 1 Date	$\dfrac{RM}{2}$ x 2 Date	$\dfrac{RM}{2}$ x 3 Date	RM Test 2 Date
1					
2					
3					
4					
5					
6					
7					
8					
9					
10					
No. of Reps.					
Exer. Time					
Pulse (HR/10 sec)					

RM   = Repetition Maximum
Pulse = 1 - before exercise; 2 - immediately after exercise; 3 - 1 min after exercise;
        4 - 2 min after exercise.

The achieved exercising time for one lap is multiplied by the number

Table 7   Performance record card for circuit training with target time and exercising without a pause.

Name: Age:
                                         Height:
                                         Weight:

Exercise	RM Test 1 Date	$\frac{RM}{2}$ x 1/t Date	$\frac{RM}{2}$ x 2/t Date	$\frac{RM}{2}$ x 3/t Date	RM Test 2 Date
1					
2					
3					
4					
5					
6					
7					
8					
9					
10					
No. of Reps.					
Exer. Time					
Pulse (HR/10 sec)	1 2 3 4	1 2 3 4	1 2 3 4	1 2 3 4	1 2 3 4

RM = Repetition Maximum
Pulse = 1 - before exercise; 2 - immediately after exercise; 3 - 1 min after exercise; 4 - 2 min after exercise.

of laps scheduled for training. If this time is then shortened by 2-3 min, it becomes the target time. The athlete must make an effort to reduce the exercise time down to the target time within three laps.

When after a few weeks of exercising the target time has been reached, the athlete is retested over one lap. Based on this second test, a new individual training load is established using

$$\frac{3\,RM}{4}\quad or\quad \frac{RM}{2}\;.$$

After exercise time has been determined for one lap using the new training load, a new target time is again set.

Table 8   Performance score card for circuit training as designed by Morgan and Adamson (20).

Name:		Age: Height: Weight:		
Exercise	RM Test 1 (Reps.)	Exercise Load 1 (Reps.)	RM Test 2 (Reps.)	Exercise Load 2 (Reps.)
Steps (1 min.)	30	15	33	17
Squat thrusts (1 min.)	28	14	30	15
Chins	5	3	7	4
Trunk curls (1 min.)	24	12	32	16
Dumb-bell jumps (30 sec.)	14	7	20	10
Barbell curls (30 sec.)	12	6	15	8
Dumbbell squats (30 sec.)	13	7	17	9
Dips (maximal)	9	5	12	6
Rope swings (maximal)	4	2	6	3
Total	139	71	172	88
Exer. Time:	18:21 min		17:32 min	
Target time:	16:00 min		15:30 min	

RM = Repetition Maximum

Ranges of Application for Variation 2

• Sports Training Program
(a) track and field (sprinters, middle- and long-distance runners); (b) all ball games activities; (c) swimming, rowing, cycling, mountaineering, skiing.

• School Programs
The method is appropriate for the 11-plus age group. The basic permissible training load is based on

$$\frac{RM}{2} \times 3.$$

The layout of the performance record card should be similar to that for circuit training, as originally designed by Morgan and Adamson (20) and shown in Table 8.

The additional loads and variations shown below have proved of particular value in circuit training based on the endurance method.

Additional Loads

Wrist rolling	10 to 15 kg
Barbell presses	30, 35, and 40 kg
Barbell curls	30, 25, and 40 kg
Barbell swings	25, 30, and 40 kg
Wheelbarrow lifts	40 kg
Dumbbell raising sideways	2 X 4 and 2 X 6 kg
Dumbbell jumps	2 X 12.5 kg
Dumbbell squats	2 X 12.5 and 2 X 20 kg
Barbell squats	45, 50, and 55 kg

Four variations in a circuit training program:

• *Standard program (9 exercises)*	*Effect on muscles*
E1 Bench stepping (one bench on top of other)	Legs and general
E2 Squat thrusts	Legs and general

E3 Chins, with jump to horizontal   Arms, shoulders and general
   bar or beam (stretch height)

E4 Jack knife variation (hands   Abdomen
   sliding along thighs to forelegs)

E5 Dumbbell jumps, stand astride   Legs and general
   bench holding a dumbbell in
   each hand, jump on and off the
   bench

E6 Barbell swings with over-grip   Arms, shoulders and
                                         abdomen

E7 Squats, holding a dumbbell   Legs and general
   in each hand

E8 Jump and press at the parallel   Arms, shoulders and
   bars, return to starting position   general
   and repeat

E9 Rope swings, without chin-ups,   Arms, shoulders and
   with push-off in vertical position   abdomen

- *Advanced program (9 exercises)*

E1 Bench or box stepping with   Legs and general
   sandbag

E2 Dumbbell jumps, stand astride   Legs and general
   bench holding a dumbbell in
   each hand, jump on and off the
   bench

E3 Chin-ups on the beam from   Arms and shoulders
   stretched hang

E4 Jack knife   Abdomen

E5 Wheelbarrow   Back and shoulders
   (lifting variable weights with
   back and arms straight)

E6 Wrist rolling   Arms, wrists, shoulders
                                         and chest

E7 Deep squats with barbell   Legs
   behind neck

E8 Pumping at parallel bars with   Arms, shoulders and
   and without swinging   abdomen

E9 Rope swings, chin-ups without   Arms, shoulders and

    pushing feet off in vertical   abdomen
    position

• *Short program (6 exercises)*

E1 Stepping on box	Legs and general
E2 Chin-ups with jump-off	Arms and shoulders
E3 Jack knife variation	Abdomen
E4 Dumbbell squats with over-grip	Arms, shoulders, and abdomen
E5 Jump and press at parallel bars	Arms, shoulders, general
E6 Rope swings	Arms, shoulders, and abdomen

• *Long program (12 exercises)*

E1 Stepping on box or bench	Legs and general
E2 Bench jumps, stand astride long bench holding dumbbell in each hand and jump with legs tucked	Legs and abdomen
E3 Chin-ups	Arms and shoulders
E4 Jack knife	Abdomen
E5 Dumbbell raising sideways to shoulder height	Shoulders and chest
E6 Star jumps with small splits	Legs and general
E7 Wheelbarrow lifts	Back, arms, and legs
E8 Wrist rolling	Arms and shoulders
E9 Dumbbell squats holding a dumbbell in each hand	Legs
E10 Barbell press (allow the barbell to rest on the breastbone	Arms, shoulders, and chest
E11 Rope swings	Arms, shoulders, and abdomen
E12 Rope ladder climbs	Legs, arms, and abdomen

4.3   Variation 3

In this variation the student or athlete attempts to complete as many laps as possible within the standard training time set by the teacher or coach. The individual training load is set as in Variation 1. The student or athlete records the number of laps completed within the set time limit. For example, the recording of 2/8 in the performance card stands for 2 completed laps plus 8 stations, i.e., the trainee was 2 stations short of 3 laps.

Loading Alternatives

• The initial exercising time of 5 min is increased in increments of 1 min, up to a maximum of 15 min per training session.
• The standard exercise time is retained; the number of repetitions at each station is increased by 2, up to a maximum of 5 in each training session.
• The training load and the exercise time remain unchanged; the number of laps is increased from, for example, 2/8 to 3/2 or 3/5. This variation is particularly suitable for school programs.

Ranges of Application

• Sports Training Programs
  (a) track and field (sprinters, middle- and long-distance runners, jumpers, javelin throwers; (b) all ball games; (c) boxing, cycling, rowing, skiing, mountaineering. For these athletes the aim is to achieve progressive increase in load to 75% of maximum performance ability.

• School Programs
  For the 12-plus age group, individual training load of

$$\frac{RM}{2} \quad \text{or} \quad \frac{3\,RM}{4}$$

may be introduced together with performance record cards as shown in Table 9.

This type of circuit training can be scheduled into any school les-

Table 9   Performance record card.

Name:		Age: Height: Weight:	
Exercise	RM Test 1	Standard 3 x	$\dfrac{RM}{4}$
1 Press-ups	20	5	
2			
3			
4			
5			
6			
7			
8			
9			
10			
No. of Reps.	200		
Exer. Time (min)		10	
No. of Laps		2/8	

RM = Repetition Maximum

son; it is particularly suitable at the beginning or the end of the lesson. Although the exercising time is of a constant duration (5 to 15 min), it allows progressive loading through the addition of laps and stations as students become more fit.

The teacher may include a mandatory rest period of 30-60 sec for all students after 3-5 min of exercising. This rest period may be eliminated if students learn to execute the exercises correctly. Exercises should under no circumstances degenerate into a mad rush from station to station. Students should be encouraged to take a breather when they feel that exercising has become too strenuous.

The advantage of using standard exercise time lies in its uncomplicated timekeeping. This allows the instructor to keep a constant watch over the exercise flow. In addition, students may take their score cards from station to station and find out how many repetitions they must do. At the end of the standard exercise time only the number of circuits and stations are recorded on the score cards. This eliminates the need for recording the repetitions at the individual stations.

Every four weeks a maximum performance score test (using 30 sec of exercising, 30 sec of rest) is carried out over one lap at each station. The new values represent the basis for setting the new training load.

Summary

All variations of the endurance circuit training method are essentially based on original circuit training designed by Morgan and Adamson (18). Simple exercises should be selected. Very demanding exercises that permit only few repetitions (e.g., chin-ups) should be avoided and replaced by easier forms (e.g., by chin-ups from a balance support hang or chin-ups from a jump-off position).

At the beginning of circuit training in schools the training load should be not higher than half the maximal repetitions. The demand may then be increased according to the particular circumstances using the suggested loading alternatives. To avoid bottlenecks at individual stations, it is imperative in all variations of circuit training based on the endurance method that the number of exercise stations exceeds the number of performers.

In sports training all variations, particularly the original forms of circuit training, can be applied. In sports training, 50 to 90% of the maximal repetitions are valid training loads.

The circuit training based on the endurance method generates the following physiological benefits: increased cardiovascular functioning, increased capillarization, increased oxygen intake capacity, increased muscular endurance, and a greater resistance to fatigue. The positive psychological effects are related to the development of will power, increased persistence, determination, and self-motivation.

5 Circuit Training Based on the Extensive Interval Method

Circuit training based on the extensive internal method is character-ized by short rest intervals of 30-45 sec after each exercise lap. One to three laps are performed. Variations of this program include:

1. Exercising time at each station is 15 sec, followed by a rest period of 45 sec;
2. Exercising time at each station is 15 sec, followed by a rest period of 30 sec;
3. Exercising time at each station is 30 sec, followed by a rest period of 30 sec;
4. Training load of

$$\frac{RM}{2}$$

at each station without any time limit is followed by a variable rest period between 45 sec to 60 sec per station.

Loading Alternatives

a. Each variation allows a load increase from one to a maximum of three laps.
b. The number of repetitions is progressively increased from

$$\frac{RM}{2} \text{ to } \frac{RM+1}{2}, \ \frac{RM+2}{2} \text{ and } \frac{RM+3}{2}.$$

Ranges of Application

- Sports Training Program
  (a) track and field (for sprinters and middle-distance runners, jumpers and javelin throwers); (b) all ball games; (c) skiing, gymnastics, judo, boxing. For these sports general and specific circuit training programs are applicable.

- School Programs
  The first three variations are suitable for pupils of the 13-plus age group. However, only general circuit training programs are applied.

Organizing Variations 1 and 2

After the exercises of the circuit have been completely mastered and the maximum number of repetitions has been determined at each station using the maximum performance score test the individual training load is set at

$$\frac{RM}{2} \, .$$

This training load must be completed within the 15 sec, preferably at a brisk pace. Depending on the exercises selected, the teacher or coach may set rest periods at 30 sec or 45 sec. The length of the rest period depends upon the weight used for each exercise, upon the level of difficulty of the exercises, and upon the intended training effect. The greater the intensity of the work performed during the exercising time and the longer the rest period, the better the conditions for the development of power and power endurance in the novice performer. If exercises using barbells are chosen, the resistance should not exceed 50 to 60% of the maximal performance. Thus, a minimum of 15 to 20 repetitions can most likely be performed by each student in the maximum performance score test during an exercising time of 30 sec. A training load of

$$\frac{RM}{2}$$

performed rapidly for 15 sec, followed by a 45 sec rest period, contributes to developing an athlete's power. During the rest period, the lactic acid concentrations in the working muscles are partially reduced. Fatigue, however, increases progressively with each exercise. Because each new exercise is designed to work a different major muscle group, the accumulation of fatigue is slowed down. A performer is thus able to work at high levels of intensity throughout the circuit, which in turn produces an increase in an athlete's power, power endurance, and general fitness. Students in the 12-14 age group should not be required to perform their individually determined training load of

$$\frac{RM}{2}$$

at a maximum speed, although it is advisable that they work at a brisk pace. The teacher must ensure that exercises are executed in the proper manner. Indeed, this is more important than speeding up the exercise pace.

Organizing Variation 3

This variation of circuit training requires that the performers exercise for 30 sec at each station and then rest for a 30 sec period. The exercises must be compiled with great care, and the difficulty of each exercise must be such that with an individual training load of

$$\frac{RM}{2}$$

the 30 second exercise time is used up completely or almost completely. Furthermore, the performance of the exercises should be unhurried and technically accurate. A training program may, therefore, consist mainly of body weight exercises with or without additional weight. These exercises permit at least 20 to 30 repetitions for maximum performance score test performed at a fast exercising pace. A training load of

$$\frac{RM}{2}$$

exercised at a steady pace requires approximately 30 sec. This basic training load can thus be easily increased progressively from lap to lap as follows:

Table 10   Sample circuit-training program with increasing exercise load over four week period.

Week	Lesson	Exercise Load (Reps.)	No. of Laps	Exercise Time from ... to (min of the lesson)
1	1	RM Test 1		30 to 45
	2	$\dfrac{RM}{2}$	x 1	1 to 15
2	1	$\dfrac{RM}{2}$	x 2	1 to 20, or 20 to 40
	2	$\dfrac{RM}{2}$	x 1	1 to 15
3	1	$\dfrac{RM}{2}$	x 3	5 to 40
	2	$\dfrac{RM}{2}$	x 1	1 to 15
4	1	RM Test 2		30 to 45
	2	$\dfrac{RM}{2}$	x 1	1 to 15

RM = Repetition Maximum

$\dfrac{RM + 1}{2}$ for lap 1, $\dfrac{RM + 2}{2}$ for lap 2, $\dfrac{RM + 3}{2}$ for lap 3.

The teacher may prescribe these increases for all the students in a class or only for individual pupils.

A sample circuit training program over four weeks is shown in Table 10. It should be evident that circuit training can be effectively

Table 11   Sample performance record card.

Name: Age:

Height::

Weight::

Exercise	RM Test 1 Date	$\dfrac{RM + 1}{2}$ x 1 Date	$\dfrac{RM + 2}{2}$ x 2 Date	$\dfrac{RM + 3}{2}$ x 3 Date	RM Test 2 Date
1					
2					
3					
4					
5					
6					
7					
8					
9					
10					
No. of Reps.					
Exer. Time					
Pulse (HR/10 sec)	1 2 3 4	1 2 3 4	1 2 3 4	1 2 3 4	1 2 3 4

RM = Repeition Maximum

used in any P.E. class. If it is well organized enough time remains available for teaching of other forms of activity. The individual instructor may include this form of circuit training at the beginning or end of the class. The maximum performance score test, however, should as a rule be always at the end of the lesson. Experience in the

use of circuit training in schools shows that students adapt themselves
quickly if they begin exercising at

$$\frac{RM}{2} \times 1$$

at the beginning of a lesson, when it serves as a warm-up period so
necessary for any training. Each instructor should decide on the particular way of including circuit training in his class time.

Organizing Variation 4

Its simple organizational arrangement makes this variation of circuit
training of particular value in physical education classes and in sports
training sessions. The maximum performance score test is carried out
as usual. The training load in the form of

$$\frac{RM}{2} \quad \text{or} \quad \frac{3\,RM}{2}$$

is done without any time limit, with the emphasis on a brisk exercise
pace and correct technique of execution. The total time spent at any
one station should amount to 45 sec or 60 sec. Anyone who completes
his or her training load requirement may relax or loosen up during the
remaining time. The instructor or coach signals the beginning of exercising at the next station. As mentioned before, tape recorders have
been found to be very useful for this type purpose. Music is played
while exercising and the sound volume is turned down briefly every
45 or 60 sec. A distinct signal announces the beginning of exercising
each time. Experience in sports training and gym classes has shown
that, when accompanied by music general fitness training always produces good results.

Summary

Their standard exercise and rest times make variations of circuit training based on the extensive interval method particularly well suited to
school sports. Since order must be maintained at each station and
when changing stations, the instructor can follow the action more
closely. The rest periods guarantee that the exercising is in keeping
with the ability of the adolescent body. Overexertion does not occur

Table 12   Sample performance record card.

Name: Age:
                                                   Height::
                                                   Weight::

Exercise Test 1	RM 2 Date	$\dfrac{RM}{2}$ x 1 Date	$\dfrac{RM}{2}$ x 2 Date	$\dfrac{RM}{2}$ x 3 Date	RM Test 2 Date	$\dfrac{RM}{2}$ x 1 Date
1						
2						
3						
4						
5						
6						
7						
8						
9						
10						
No. of Reps.						
Exer. Time						
Pulse (HR/10 sec)						

RM   = Repetition Maximum
Pulse = 1 - before exercise; 2- immediately after exercise; 3 -1 min after exercise;
        4 - 2 min after exercise.

when training at the

$$\frac{RM}{2} \text{ x } 3$$

training load. Exercising with short rest intervals ensures the proper development of physical fitness. Not only does the extensive interval method develop general endurance, but also improves complex fitness-related abilities, power endurance, muscular endurance, and maximal strength. It is not permissible to increase the training load by shortening the rest periods. This would distort the character of circuit training and its related training effect when it is based on the extensive interval method. In circuit-training programs in school, exercises using body weight only are most popular. Many of them allow the use of an additional load, such as medicine ball, sandbag, horizontal bar, and so on. Athletes in competitive sport may use body weight exercises with or without additional weight (barbell, weighted jacket, sand bag, etc).

Sample performance cards for circuit training based on the extensive interval method are shown in Tables 11 and 12.

The circuit training based on the extensive interval method generates the following physiological benefits: increased cardiovascular functioning, increased capillarization, increased oxygen absorption capacity, and increased aeorbic capacity. The physical benefits of this type of training are: increased general endurance, increased power, and increased muscular endurance. The psychological benefits are related to the development of will power, increased self-confidence, increased motivation, and dedication for training.

6 Circuit Training Based on the Intensive Interval Method

The nature of the intensive interval training method determines the organization of circuit training and its execution. The exercises should be compiled in such a way that it is possible for the athlete to do only 8-12 repetitions during a standard exercise time of 10-15 sec or to complete approximately 8-12 repetitions without any time limit. From a program of ten exercises at least five must be done with additional weights. The additional loading may consist of standard or constant resistance (medicine balls, horizontal bars, round weights, and sandbags) or of variable or gradable resistance (barbells, dumbbells, weighted cuffs, weighted jackets, etc). The length of the rest periods between the individual set of exercises may vary between 30 and 90 sec. After each lap the rest period is 3-5 min. Explosive and technically precise execution is a prime consideration for all variations of circuit training based on the intensive interval method.

Two variations of circuit training based on the intensive interval method are suggested and are discussed below.

6.1 Variation 1

Exercising at each station for 10-15 sec at each station is followed by a rest period lasting between 30-90 sec. The length of the rest period depends on the intensity of the work performed using a resistance of approximately 75% of the maximal performance and on the intended training effect.

As a loading alternative for this variation, the exercise time may be reduced from 15 sec to 10 sec. The 8-12 repetitions must be completed with precision and at a continuously increasing pace. The set rest period should not be shortened. As soon as the number of repetitions per set have been mastered in the reduced exercising time, a maximum performance score test should be carried out. This test forms the basis for setting a new training load at 75% resistance of the current maximal performance.

As a rule, this variation of circuit training requires: (a) no increase in the number of repetitions per set; and (b) rest periods that are not shortened.

This variation produces excellent development of power (rest period of up to 90 sec for each series), power endurance, and muscular endurance (rest period of 30-45 sec).

6.2   Variation 2

Each exercise is repeated from 8 to a maximum of 12 times without any time limit, but at a quick pace. The length of the rest period is a minimum of 30 sec and a maximum of 180 sec. As in variation 1, each exercise is carried out at approximately 75% resistance of the maximal performance. The rest period is suitable for limbering-up and stretching exercises, which are very important in achieving the desired training effect.

In another version of this variation, the total load is increased as in variation 1. However, no standard exercising time is specified. The tempo is brisk and/or sub-maximal. Exercise time for each set of 8-12 repetitions may be measured and compared from set to set or from one training session to another. This provides an excellent way of gaining an insight into fitness development. As in body building, the exercises are carried out in three parallel sets, i.e., all sets at one station are completed first before the athlete moves on to the next exercise station. There is a rest period of approximately 60-120 sec after each set of exercises. This promotes the development of maximal strength in addition to the development of power.

The following training program based on the intensive interval method may serve as an example.

Exercises	*Rest Period Activity*
E1 Clean	Arm rotations backward

		(clean weight and replace)
E2	Snatching	Trunk curls in seated stretch position with back straight
E3	Jerking	Hanging on wall bars (jerk and replace)
E4	Squats	Cycling (weight behind neck)
E5	Bench press	Hanging and slight chinning
E6	Sit-ups from supine position with back straight and sandbag behind neck	Backward trunk bends
E7	Standing snatch or dumbbell swinging	Straddle sitting position - forward trunk bends
E8	Twisted trunk curls,	Straddle sitting position - seated or standing trunk curls to side
E9	Jumping jack	Curling on the wall bars
E10	Single-leg jumps on the bench with sandbag (5 times left, 5 times right)	Shoulder support, leg kicking

The maximum performance score test is carried out before beginning training according to the existing training program. Individual training load or individual resistance training is then expressed in terms of the percentage of maximal performance score, as shown in Table 13.

Ranges of application

• Sports Training Program
(a) track and field (variation 1 for sprinters and jumpers; variation 2 for shot-putters, throwers, jumpers); (b) all types of ball games (variation 1); (c) gymnastics (variation 2), (d) boxing (variation 1); (e) judo (variations 1 and 2).

• School Programs
12-18 age group. The loads from

$$\frac{RM}{2} \text{ up to } \frac{3\,RM}{4}$$

are applicable in exercises with standard resistances added to the body weight exercises. This includes medicine ball, sandbag (10 to 15 kg), horizontal bar, gymnastic bench, weights (10-15 kg) and another partner of approximately equal weight. Variation 1 is particularly suitable for training programs in schools, i.e., 10-15 sec standard exercising is followed by a standard rest period of 30-45 sec. Variation 2 can also be used. Care must especially be taken here that students are required only to exercise at a brisk pace and that they are not timed for each set, which would create undue complications.

Organization of Program

Once the athletes have mastered the exercises, they should become acquainted with the organization of the circuit. The introduction is then followed by the first maximum performance score test, as in variations of circuit training described previously. The training levels amount to approximately 50 to 75% of the maximal performance. For school programs individual training levels of

$$\frac{RM}{2} \text{ up to } \frac{3\,RM}{4}$$

may be established. For sports training, as for school programs, this form of circuit training may be organized in the following ways, depending upon the variation used:

• The exercises compiled in accordance with the circuit training logo are executed in sequence, one after the other, in one to three laps (classic system of circuit training).

• All sets of each exercise are completed first before moving on to the next station (parallel sets), that is, the first set of exercise one is followed by the second and third sets of exercise 1, with a rest between each set. After the rest, the athlete proceeds to station 2 and performs all sets of exercise 2, and so on. This type of training scheme corresponds to the bodybuilding system. The three sets performed one after the other make more intensive demands on the working muscle group. The local fatigue confined to the particular muscle group builds more rapidly from set to set, so that the selected training levels of approximately 75% of the maximal performance repre-

Table 13   Exercise loading or resistance scheme.

Week	Resistance (% of 1 RM)	Repetition (n)
1	50	10
2	60	10
3	65	8 to 10
4	70	8
5	75	6

sent almost a maximal load by the third set. The muscular group concerned does not get active recovery until the athlete has changed to the next exercise station. As a result of the relatively long rest period after each series, the cardiac, circulatory, and respiratory systems undergo no more strenuous activity than in the variations of circuit training described earlier, as a result of the relatively long rest period after each series. In spite of this, the training nevertheless has still quite a considerable effect on the cardiac, circulatory, and respiratory systems: it improves metabolic activity in particular and increases the buffer capacity, resulting in the development of maximal strength, muscular endurance and, especially, power endurance.

When doing circuit training based on the intensive interval method for competitive training and school sports, exercising should be organized differently from the variations described above. Simplicity is essential. The nature of variations 1 and 2 with regard to exercise duration and number of repetitions remains the same, because at any at any one station, all of the athletes or students are no longer exercising simultaneously. For school sports we recommend that every two or three students exercise in sequence at each station. Each student completes his or her set (approximately 8-12 repetitions) at a rapid pace. Exercise time is between 10 and 15 sec. This set-up roughly allows for the first variation to be performed with three students per station, and makes for effective and enjoyable exercising. It is also very effective for allowing students to monitor each other (verifying the number of repetitions, observing exercise execution, and so on). There is another advantage: only one exercise location and one piece

Table 14   Sample performance record card for circuit training based on the intensive interval method.

Name: Age:
                                        Height::
                                        Weight::

Exercise	RM Test 1 Date	3 x 10/ t Date	3 x 10/ t Date	3 x 10/ t Date	RM Test 2 Date
1					
2					
3					
4					
5					
6					
7					
8					
9					
10					
No of Reps.					
Total kg					
Total kgm					
kgm/sec					
Pulse (HR/10 sec.)	2 1 3 4	2 1 3 4	2 1 3 4	2 1 3 4	2 1 3 4

of apparatus is required for three students; this is especially important for schools that have little in the way of equipment. Rest period activity is especially important. Students must never sit down during the rest period, but do simple loosening-up exercises instead.

In sports training, the program is composed mainly of barbell exercises. Three or four athletes should share one barbell; it is unimportant whether variation 1 or 2 is used. Even if the coach does not record the time, the right physiological balance between exercising and resting (or exertion and relaxation) is established (the coach may, of course, use a stop watch). Practice has shown, however, that this is only feasible with a squad consisting of 3-4 athletes. The coach should ensure that the rest period is used for stretching and limbering exercises (see rest period exercises E1a-E10a on pp. 187 and 189) at all times.

Summary

Circuit training based on the intensive interval method differs from the circuit training variations described thus far. This is because of the physiological effects which this method produces. The students or athletes no longer exercise all at the same time, but in groups of two to four, one after the other. This circuit training program establishes a unique balance between exercise and recovery that generates positive physical and psychological training effects. A sample performance record card is shown in Table 14.

The physiological effects are related to the improved metabolism, buffer capacity and energy potential, and an increased anaerobic capacity. The physical training effects are related to the increased maximal strength, better muscular endurance, and improved power endurance. The psychological benefits result in improved concentration, development of will power, better self-confidence, increased motivation, and a greater readiness to take risks.

7 Circuit Training Based on the Repetition Method

Repetition circuit training is performed almost exclusively by using weights of variable resistance, such as barbells and dumbbells. The stimulus intensity or resistance for each exercise amounts to approximately 80% and up to above 90% (occasionally as much as 100%) of the maximal performance capacity. In addition to the well-known classic weightlifting exercises, clean and jerk and snatching (with or without split or squat technique), many other exercises using dumbbells may be used: deep squats, half squats, cleans, one-armed jerking and snatching, pressing; lifting the dumbbell with arms and back straight in front of the body, to the side and behind the body, and between legs astride; jumping jack; three-count exercises, and so on.

Exercising at or near maximal resistance levels means that only a low number of repetitions is possible, normally no more than three in one set. Research (16) has shown that lifts in the range of 80-90% of the maximal performance must be followed by rest periods lasting from 2 to 3 min, and in the 90-100% range, between 3 to 5 min. Excessive shortening or lengthening of the suggested rest periods will produce poor results.

According to research conducted in the Soviet Union (16, 17, 28), the best training results for the development of maximal strength is achieved by exercising at moderate to high levels (70-90%) of resistance and with 3-4 repetitions per set (see Table 15). Roman (25) considers the training method presented in Table 16 to be effective. He also holds the view that athletes should only occasionally be asked to do lifts in the absolute maximal range (100% resistance). The current fitness level of the athlete must always be taken into consideration when planning the training levels using circuit training based on the

Table 15   Positive training effect as a function of variable resistance training.

Training Load (in % of 1 RM)	Improvement in strength			Total Improvement
	Jerking kg	Snatching kg	Pressing kg	kg
45 to 60	8.6	4.1	3.9	16.6
60 to 75	9.7	5.3	5.9	20.0
70 to 90	10.8	9.4	7.7	27.9

repetition method.

The following training method for repetition circuit training is based on studies conducted by several Soviet sports specialists. This method, which is supported by investigations conducted by German writers, has had a positive effect on the development of maximal strength and power. The weight levels for each exercise are such that eight repetitions can be done within the first set. For every set thereafter the weight is gradually increased (by approximately 5 kg per set), thus allowing the athletes to perform only 6, 4, then 2, and finally only 1 repetition per set. Each set is followed by a rest period of 90 to 120 sec. At maximal levels (approximately 95-100% resistance) four single lifts are performed with a constant rest period of 2 min between each lift. The weight is then gradually decreased, with the number of repetitions per set being increased from 2 to 4 and finally to 6. The

Table 16   Training method according to Roman (24).

Training Load (in %/1 RM)	No. of Sets (n)	Repetitions Per Set (n)
Approx. 80 to 90	5 to 7, or	4
	6 to 8	3
Approx. 85 to 90	5 to 6	2
80 and 90, alternating	6 to 8	3

Table 17   Strength training using the pyramid system.

Exercise	S1	S2	S3	S4	S5	S6	S7	S8	S9	S10	S11
	P	P	P	P	P	P	P	P	P	P	
	8R	6R	4R	2R	1R	1R	1R	1R	2R	4R	6R
Snatch											
Press											
Jerk												
Squat												

S - Set; R - Repetition; P - Pause

application of this method as a variation of circuit training is shown in Table 17.

This form of exercising, often referred as pyramid system of strength training, may be regarded as variation of circuit training since the exercises chosen (for example snatch, clean, jerk, and deep squats bends) can be done one after the other. The program was tried over 4 weeks with a group of four athletes, who attended training sessions once a week. Each athlete was trying to reduce the lifting time for each set. A control group of five athletes exercised without having their time monitored. The results of the maximum strength test indicated that the test group demonstrated better improvement than the control group. We recommend three variations of circuit training based on the repetition method for the development of power and maximal strength. They are presented below.

7.1   Variation 1

The initial loading allows 8 repetitions per set for each exercise. Rest periods between series are 120 sec long, during which time stretching and loosening-up activities are done. Lifting time is timed for each set. Weight and exercise choice remain the same.

• Objective
  To reduce the lifting times per set.

- Loading alternatives
  A maximum performance score test is carried out before the standard weight can be lifted within an even shorter time. Based on the results, the new weight loads for the pyramid, or 8, 6, 4, 2, 1, 2, 4, and 6 repetitions are determined.

7.2   Variation 2

The standard lifting time is 10 to 15 sec. The weight to be lifted for the first set is fixed at 50% of the maximal performance per exercise. This resistance then increases from 50% to 60%, 70%, and three times at 80%. The resistance then decreases to 70%, 60%, and finally to 50%. The number of repetitions achieved within the standard lifting time is recorded on the score card. Stretching and limbering-up exercises are done during the rest periods that should last between 90 and 180 seconds.

- Objective
  To increase the number of repetitions within the standard exercise time.

- Loading alternatives
  If the number of repetitions within the standard lifting time cannot be increased, a maximum performance score test is conducted, providing the basis for new individual loading values of 50%, 60%, 70%, and 80%.

7.3   Variation 3

The selected exercises are done one after the other. The rest period between each set should last between 80 and 180 seconds depending on the intensity of exercising. The rest period serves for stretching and limbering up of fatigued muscles.

For each exercise the total number of repetitions is 8, 6, 4, 2, 1, 4, and 6. Lifting times are not recorded.

- Objective

To achieve the required number of repetitions for each exercise despite an increase in the weight loads. A second maximum performance score test is performed during the fourth training week.
- Loading alternatives
  The weight load of each exercise and each set is increased by 2.5 to 5 kg every week, taking into account the current level of fitness.

Ranges of application

- Sports Training Programs
  a) Track and field (variations 1 to 3 for shot-putters and throwers, and variations 1 and 2 for jumpers and sprinters); b) boxing (variations 1 to 3); c) ball games (variations 1 and 2); d) winter sports (variation 1 and 3 for alpine and jumping events); and e) rowing (variations 1 and 3), gymnastics (variation 3).

- School Programs
  Repetition circuit training is not suitable for physical education programs in schools.

Organization of the Training Session

Since it is difficult for coaches to record lifting times and rest periods for a large group of athletes, the training may therefore be organized as follows: three to four athletes should be set to exercise, one after the other, on any one set of dumbbells. It is advisable to set the groups up according to their performance levels. Each exercise group needs a stop watch so that its members can record each other's lifting times. It is not necessary to time the rest periods, since separate experiments have shown that when three athletes are exercising one after the other, the rest period is always approximately 90 sec; for four athletes approximately 90-120 sec. When exercising using variation 2, the coach may give the signal for everyone to begin exercising or lifting at the same time.

In variation 3, the length of the rest periods must be kept the same. Each group of athletes is given a stop watch for this purpose. (A wrist watch can also be used.)

It is vital that the athletes record the performance achieved on cards in the manner shown in Table 18 for all three variations.

Table 18   Sample performance record card for body-building with dumbbells using pyramid system.

Name:					Age:							
					Height:							
					Weight:							

	S1 8R	Lifting time(t) (sec)	S2 t 6R	S3 t 4R	S4 t 2R	S5 t 1R	S6 t 1R	S7 t 2R	S8 t 4R	S9 t 6R
Snatch	50 kg	55								
Press	50 kg	30								
Jerk	55 kg	40								
Squat	55kg	45								
Total	1700 kg/32R									
kg/R	53									
kg/sec	10									
Exer. Time (sec)		170								
Total Performance:		8575 kg/136R								
Total Time: 12:10 min										
Lifting Performance: 18 kg/sec										

Summary

The high resistance levels of training and the complexity of application make circuit training based on the repetition method suitable for sports training, in which a relatively small number of athletes train for competition. It is not recommended for use in school programs.

The physiological effects of this circuit training method are related to enlargement of the muscle cross-section, improved sensory-motor coordination of weight lifting, and greater energy potential.

The physical training effects are related to increased maximal strength and increased power and power endurance. The psychological effects are improved will power, readiness to take risks, greater dedication and motivation for training, ability to improve performance, and increased self-confidence.

8 Organization and Implementation of Circuit Work

We recommend that children 9 to 10 years of age exercise in groups by using *station work*. This method serves to develop and strengthen the various movement skills that form the basis for circuit training in later years. Well-organized station work in classes for pupils of the 9-10 age group (see station work on pp. 163-165) is a good way to introduce circuit training, which should be used as a standard procedure in general fitness training for school sports. Depending on the effort necessary to accomplish the main exercise, the student may be required to do several relevant supplementary exercises. As a principal method of exercising, the teacher may use the repetition method based on standard or varied conditions. The method adopted depends on the nature of the exercise program.

It should also be noted that the structuring and the duration of the rest periods depend on the nature of each exercise, whether, for example, that exercise involved a sub-maximal, medium, or low application of resistance and high or low requirements of concentration.

Exercising performed in groups results in greater density of training. In addition to strengthening the movement skills, it is therefore possible to improve the coordination needed for those skills. It does not matter whether movement skills are consolidated by using repetitions under standard or varied conditions. Only those exercise methods that ensure the development of exercise-specific movement characteristics by means of proper interaction between exercise and recovery should be chosen.

After a few sessions using station work, the *circuit work* method is introduced as the next logical step in preparation for circuit training. The transition from station work to circuit work and circuit training implies, as a rule, an intensification of physical education lessons and a more purposeful development of physical abilities.

8.1   Circuit Work Based on the Endurance Method and the Extensive Interval Method

To develop the fitness-related abilities in the 10-11 age group, we recommend circuit work based on the endurance method or on the extensive interval method. In both instances care must be taken that training levels and recovery are well balanced. Hasenkruger (8) suggests that the goal of this training method should be to achieve a certain amount of work in the shortest period of time, or to accomplish a high volume of work within a specified time. He even suggests circuit work with no rest period and completing the program in three laps with the maximal number of repetitions. He concedes, however, that this approach may lead to overexertion and monotony. He therefore suggests that this type of very intensive circuit work only be performed from time to time.

The following procedure is recommended for circuit work based on the endurance method. The program should consist of 10 strength exercises taken from track-and-field or from other sports with an aim to develop either general or specific fitness. The individual stations should be well marked, as discussed previously in Chapter 3. The groups (consisting of a maximum of 5 students) are distributed among the 10 stations so as to leave two stations vacant at the beginning of the lesson. The group leader determines the order of the exercise sequence, leading the group to any one of the vacant stations in order to avoid congestion. When exercises at one station are completed, the group leader writes the squad's number on the floor or on a piece of paper supplied for this purpose at each station as corroborating evidence. To give the students a better idea of what is involved, the teacher may wish to illustrate the exercise program on the blackboard.

The number of repetitions performed at each station should be kept very low, and within the range of average performance (for instance, maximal push-up repetitions for 10-year-old students is approximately 25; the average class result is approximately 8; therefore the number of repetitions demanded is set at 8). This ensures that exercising is done using the endurance method and thus without any rest period, except for the break that must be taken when changing stations.

The teacher should encourage groups to compete against each other, to determine, for example, which squad can complete a single lap in the shortest possible time while executing all the exercises accurately.

At this level, score cards are not used. However, the times accomplished (for one up to three laps) should be recorded on a blackboard and should then be entered in the group diary by the group leader. This type of circuit training can be changed in each lesson. If, however, the program has proven itself to be very useful, it should be retained for six lessons. As in circuit training, the loading should be increased progressively from lesson to lesson and from week to week (see Table 19). If the number of laps is increased to two or even three, there should be a rest of at least 2 to 3 min between each lap. The teacher may wish to use the rest period for instruction in technique, or to introduce pulse measurement (practise at this early age so that pulse measurement will not be novel or unusual to students with the introduction of circuit training). The main advantage of this variation of circuit training is that students are kept active and learn to become independent and self-reliant. In addition, it fosters team spirit and helps to develop leadership skills in the group leader.

It should be noted that students of this age group are eager to perform; exercises should be packed as densely as possible. Interest in the circuit work program can usually be sustained by increasing the number of laps from one to three and, again, by encouraging competition between the groups. Comparative results (recorded in the group's diary) for improvements in performance also help motivate students.

Table 19   Sample circuit work program showing an increase in training load.

Week 1		Week 2		Week 3
Lesson	No. of Laps	Lesson	No. of Laps	New Programme
1	1	1	1	
2	2	2	2	
3	3	3	3	

Any significant disadvantages that are apparent in this form of circuit work cease to exist under real circuit training conditions. Still, the most noticeable disadvantage is that all pupils are required to do the same number of repetitions at individual stations. Pupil A may feel that the established training load is too low, while pupil B may find it is just right, and pupil C may believe it is too much. We shall therefore continue to speak of circuit work and not refer to circuit training until after the loading is allotted individually. Besides, as students are allowed to choose the exercise sequence themselves, there is no guarantee that the main muscle groups will be exercised alternately according to the circuit training logo.

The absence of the score cards precludes any exact evidence of the improvement of performance ability. It would, however, be too early to hand out record cards to pupils in the 10-11 age group.

The organization and methodology of circuit work by the extensive interval method is similar to those used in circuit work by the endurance method. However, exercises based on the principle of the extensive interval method involve a different loading characteristic. Changing stations after exercising without haste for 15-30 sec, and resting for 30 seconds, for example, produces good results. With all the students beginning the exercises at the same time and resting at the same time, the sequence of exercises flows smoothly. In classes with discipline problems, the instructor may begin by having the students march from one station to the other in a strict order, following commands given by the teacher or by the group leader at each station. Absolute adherence to the length of rest periods is not of paramount importance; order and discipline, combined with high dedication to performance during the exercising phase, are. In classes where good discipline and earnest cooperation prevail, strict order still has its place. However, in keeping with the objective of promoting self-discipline and independence, the signals to change stations should be given by the group leader.

Exercise programs with 6-10 stations are best suited for circuit work using the extensive interval method. The following rule applies: the fewer the number of stations, the greater the number of exercise facilities need be available. The instructor must realize that it is easier to equip more, that is, ten exercise stations and have only three students exercising at each station than it is to have a large number of students exercising at a relatively small number of stations, where students may obstruct each other.

If only six stations are available, arrangements should be made for three students to do exercises while the others take a break. The student not exercising can

1. help those doing exercises,
2. count the number of repetitions, or
3. correct technique and offer any other relevant suggestions.

8.2   Circuit Work Based on the Intensive Interval Method

The intensive interval method can also be applied to circuit work. A good balance between loading and recovery can be achieved by ensuring that the stations are well marked, as they are for the endurance method. The squads (consisting of a maximum of 6 students) are divided up among the individual stations, as before. However, all six squad members do not exercise at one time. Rather, they take turns; that is, when some students exercise the others sit out, taking a break. Every exercise should be repeated 8 to 10 times, the repetitions being counted by the students who are sitting out. When everyone has completed the first exercise, each squad moves on to the next station and begins the exercise in the previously arranged order. The change from one station to the next should be made in one specified direction. Congestion can be avoided if athletes are assigned to eight of, say, ten available stations. Continued congestion may indicate unsuitable exercises or a lack of balance between exercises. Exercises that cause bottlenecks should be replaced. The change between exercising and recovery is related to the intensive interval method. A standard exercise time at each station is unnecessary if all the required sets are completed before moving on to the next station.

Each set is followed by a short rest period, which occurs when squad members take their turns in exercising. The sample programs outlined in Table 20 will help show the progressive increase in training.

Students must constantly be reminded that even with increased number of sets, they still have to perform the same number of repetitions. In order to induce students to take a rest, have them do various exercises involving a partner (see pp. 157-162).

Table 20   Sample circuit training program showing a progressive increase in training load throughout the week.

Week	Lesson	Program 1 No. of Laps	Program 2 No. of Sets per Exer. Station
1	1	1	1 x 10
	2	2	2 x 10
	3	3	3 x 10
2	1	1	1 x 10
	2	2	2 x 10
	3	3	3 x 10
3	1 new program commences	1	1 x 10

Circuit work based on the intensive interval method should not take the form of a competition for the fastest time of performing a lap. This would certainly disrupt the scheduled rest between exercises.

Exercising with intensive strength component for 10 to 20 sec, without any quota set for repetitions, has also proved to be successful in circuit work by the intensive interval method in school sports programs for the 12-plus age group. Rest periods are self-regulating when students are taking turns one after the other. There is a ratio of 10:20, 15:30 or 20:40 sec exercising to recovery time with 3 pupils exercising in succession, based on the exercise time of 10, 15, or 20 sec, as set by the teacher. Those not exercising should be used as assistants, observers, and recorders.

At this level performance record cards for compiling individual performance should not be used. The following suggestions will help motivate students to improve their performance:

• Application of exercises with a clear starting and finishing position to permit easy counting.

• Comparisons of the performances of individual students must aim at objectivity.

- Record cards should be introduced only after the program has been carried out several times (4 to 6 times) over a period of 2 to 6 weeks.

- The same exercise sequence should be retained in all subsequent classes.

Summary

Circuit work for the 10-11 age group using the variations described in this chapter may, of course, also be applied to higher age groups. Indeed, if the students have no previous experience with fitness-related training they should be prepared for circuit training by doing appropriate type of circuit training work over a number of weeks. The exercises chosen by the teacher for circuit work may also be used for later circuit training (with the exception of those exercises that cannot be done individually and that cannot be measured accurately within circuit training).

Circuit work designed as preparatory training for circuit training has the following training-related effects: it enhances the complex development of selected fitness abilities, mainly related to power and power endurance.

9   Circuit Training Using Partner Exercises

As a variation, exercises using partners, as shown on pages 156-161, are also effective in circuit training. Young athletes find these exercises particularly enjoyable, and they require no equipment. They are therefore suitable for school programs, particularly those with large numbers of students. Unlike some other programs, circuit training using partner exercises may be performed outdoors. These exercises also permit useful alternation between isotonic and isometric muscular work when partners change the roles within each exercise. Inspection of Figures 167-198 in Section 4, pp. 156-161, should reveal clearly the part of the exercise combination that is linked with isotonic or isometric muscular work. The duration of the stimulus both for isotonic and isometric exercising can be established by using a standard exercise time of 6, 8, 10, or 12 sec. The objective in this type of circuit training is to increase the number of repetitions within the given exercise when working isotonically. The repetitions are then recorded on a performance record card which is used for monitoring individual progress (see sample performance card in Table 21). Choose no more than ten partner exercises for a circuit training program.

For circuit training using partner exercises the following variations can be used:

- The students exercise one after the other; the entire program is carried out in three laps. Each exercise is followed by a rest period, which results when partners changing roles. The rest periods between the individual laps are set at 2 to 3 min.

- Each partner exercise is conducted in succession. Both partners

Table 21   Sample performance record card. Exercise time is set at 10
               sec per exercise set.

Name: Age:

                                 Height:

                                 Weight:

Exercise	Date			Date			Date			Date		
	Laps			Laps			Laps			Laps		
	1 R	2 R	3 R	1 R	2 R	3 R	1 R	2 R	3 R	1 R	2 R	3 R
2	8	7	8	8	8	8						
3	10	9	7	10	10	9						
4	6	7	5	6	6	6						
5	7	7	5	7	8	7						
6	4	5	4	5	6	5						
1	6	7	5	6	6	6						
9	8	8	8	8	8	8						
10	1	1	1	1	1	1						
7	6	5	4	6	6	5						
8	8	7	7	9	7	7						
R	90	89	78	93	91	86						
Time(s)	100	100	100	100	100	100						
Total R/	257			270								
Exer. Time(s)	300			300								

R = Repetitions

change roles quickly without any rest period. When both partners
have completed one exercise there is a short rest period until they
commence with the next exercise. The rest period is used for record-

ing the number of repetitions on the performance record cards and time for relaxing slightly. Rest periods between individual laps are approximately 1 to 3 min long.

• Each of the ten exercise combinations is done in a series of three sets before moving on to the next exercise station. There is a short rest period between each set.

Partners should be of approximately equal height and weight. A circular arrangement is best suited for partner exercises. All pairs can perform the same exercise simultaneously. As in circuit training, it is also possible to let them move from one station to the next. The various exercising stations are numbered and each exercise is explained by a stick diagram.

Fitness improvements over time can be determined by a maximal performance score test using the same partner exercises or by using a specifically chosen test program.

10 Circuit Training Methods for Home Training

Circuit training has proved its worth in leisure and recreation sports and in individual fitness-related training at home. We shall not deal with the many variations suitable for training at home. However, here are some circuit training variations for home use that are also recommended for the so-called "short circuits" (see p. 190):

Table 22   Norms for push-ups.

Age (years)	Very Good		Good		Average	
	male	female	male	female	male	female
6	10	8	7	5	4	3
7	11	8	8	5	5	3
8	12	9	9	6	6	3
9	13	9	10	6	7	3
10	14	9	11	6	8	4
11	15	9	12	7	9	4
12	17	10	14	7	10	4
13	19	10	16	7	11	4
14	20	10	17	7	12	5
15	21	11	18	8	13	5
16	22	11	19	8	14	5
17	23	12	20	8	15	6
18	24	12	21	8	15	6

- Each exercise is done in one set with up to 30 repetitions. Each set is followed by a 1 to 2 min rest. During the rest the pulse should drop to approximately 120 beats/min. Depending on fitness level, up to three laps may be completed.

- Each exercise is executed in a series of three sets of 10 repetitions each. Each series is followed by a rest lasting 1 min.

Consult Tables 22 to 26 for fitness norms for performances in selected exercises, as proposed by Stemmler (29). By comparing his or her own performance with these norms, a student can estimate performance level and the progress made thus far.

Table 23   Norms for stretch jumps with feet together from deep squat.

Age (years)	Very Good		Good		Average	
	male	female	male	female	male	female
6	12	12	10	9	7	7
7	8	17	14	12	10	9
8	23	21	18	15	12	11
9	28	25	23	18	14	12
10	32	27	27	19	16	14
11	34	28	29	20	18	15
12	36	29	31	20	20	15
13	38	30	33	20	23	15
14	40	30	35	20	25	15
15	45	35	40	25	30	20
16	50	35	45	28	35	23
17	55	40	50	30	40	25
Additional: Single-leg squat	15	10	10	7	5	4

Table 24   Norms for chin-ups for 6-10 year-olds from inclined support hang; 11-plus age group students from high bar.

Age	Very Good		Good		Average	
(years)	male	female	male	female	male	female
6	14	10	10	7	6	3
7	17	12	13	8	8	4
8	21	14	15	10	9	5
9	25	17	18	12	10	6
10	29	20	21	12	12	6
11	5	3	4	2	3	2
12	6	3	5	2	3	2
13	6	3	5	2	3	2
14	7	3	6	2	4	2
15	7	3	6	2	4	2
16	8	3	7	2	5	2
17	9	3	8	2	6	2
18	10	3	9	2	7	2

Table 25   Norms for chin-ups for 11-plus age group from inclined support hang.

Age	Very Good		Good		Average	
(years)	male	female	male	female	male	female
11	14	10	12	8	9	6
12	14	10	12	8	9	6
13	15	13	13	10	10	7
14	15	13	13	10	10	7
15	18	15	15	12	11	7
16	18	15	15	12	11	7
17	21	17	18	14	13	8
18	21	17	18	14	13	8

Table 26   Norms for climbing a 4 m pole or rope: (6-10 year-olds are
              evaluated on the basis of m completed whereas 11-plus age
              group students are evaluated on the basis of achieved time
              in sec).

Age (years)	Very Good male	Very Good female	Good male	Good female	Average male	Average female
6	3.5 m	3.5 m	3.0 m	3.0 m	2.5 m	2.0 m
7	4.0 m	3.5 m	3.5 m	3.0 m	2.5 m	2.0 m
8	4/3 m*	4.0 m	4.0 m	3.5 m	3.0 m	2.5 m
9	2x4 m	4/3m*	4/3 m*	4.0 m	3.5 m	3.0 m
10	3x4 m	2x4 m	2x4 m	4/3 m*	4.0 m	3.0 m
11	6.7 s	7.6 s	8.0 s	10.1 s	12.0 s	4.0 m
12	6.2 s	7.1 s	7.6 s	9.6 s	10.7 s	4.0 m
13	5.8 s	6.7 s	6.7 s	9.1 s	9.3 s	4.0 m
14	5.3 s	6.2 s	6.2 s	8.6 s	8.1 s	4.0 m
15	5.1 s	5.8 s	5.9 s	8.1 s	7.1 s	4.0 m
16	4.8 s	5.3 s	5.7 s	7.7 s	6.6 s	4.0 m
17	4.5 s	5.1 s	5.4 s	7.4 s	6.1 s	4.0 m
18	4.3 s	5.0 s	5.2 s	7.1 s	5.8 s	4.0 m

*4/3: climbing 4 m once, immediately followed by climbing additional 3 m.

Table 27   Summary review of the circuit-training methods (S -Series; P - Pause; R - Repetition).

	Repetition Method	Intensive Interval Method	Extensive Interval Method	Endurance Method
Intensity of Exercise	maximal-submaximal	sub-maximal-high	high-medium	medium-low
Density of Exercise	2-5 min SP: 1-5 min after each exercise	90-180 sec SP; 30-45 sec rest after each station	670-180 sec SP; 30 sec rest after each station	no rest
Volume of Exercise	low 1-3 R/S 20-30 individual repetitions/exercise	medium 4-8 R/S 6-12 R/station	high 10-20 R/S 15-20 R/station	high — 10-40 R/Station
Duration of Exercise	brief/individual ex 5-30 sec/S 90-120 min total time	10-20 sec/S 10-60 min total time	15-30 sec/S 10-40 min total time	3-5 min/lap 10-30 min total time
Training Effect	maximal strength power	power muscular endurance	muscular endurance aerobic endurance	aerobic endurance muscular endurance
Pedagogic and Psychological Effects	impact on will power ability to call upon psychological and physiological powers	impact on will power ability to call upon psychological and physiological powers	will power resistance to fatigue	will power stamina resistance to fatigue
Physiological Effects	muscular cross section sensory-motor co-ordination energy potential	sensory/motor co-ordination energy potential metabolism	cardiovascular efficiency metabolism buffer capacity	cardiovascular efficiency aerobic capacity

Nature of Exercises	metabolism general and specific exercises with additional load	buffer capacity general and specific exercises with/without additional load	general and specific exercise with/without additional load	general and specific exercises without (with) additional load
Variations	station training: indiv. exercises or sets set training in series pyramid system 8-6-4-2-1-2-4-6-8	station and set training intensive circuit training	circuit training extensive	circuit training
Maximal Score Test	ascertaining the max. performance ability in every exercise without time limit 30 sec ex./30 sec pause	exercising with additional load RM without time limit; ex. with without add. load	30 sec exercising 30 sec rest	30 sec exercising 30 sec rest
Range of Application	• competitive training • general and specific conditioning for sports requiring strength and power • sport for all (strength oriented) • not applicable for school programs	• competitive training • general and specific conditioning for sports requiring strength, power endurance • sport for all (strength oriented) - in schools for 12-plus age group population	• competitive training • general and specific conditioning for sports requiring endurance • general conditioning sports requiring strength, speed-strength • sport for all (strength and endurance oriented) • in schools for 11-plus age group population	• competitive training • general and specific conditioning for sports requiring endurance • general conditioning sports requiring strength and speed-strength • sport for all (endurance oriented) • in schools for 11-plus age group population

11 Evaluation Practices in School Programs

Here are some hints for evaluating performance in school-age children which instructors should find useful. Although the number of repetitions can be determined accurately by a maximum performance score test, comparisons between performances are difficult to make because almost all circuit training programs are compiled differently and executed under varied conditions. The application of standard programs on county, district, and national levels could form the basis of an impartial system of evaluation. This, however, may result in too formal or rigid an appraisal. But we can make more positive recommendations for the evaluation of the performance based on our own investigations.

Do not award marks on the basis of arbitrarily established norms for any training program. The enthusiasm of weaker performers in particular is stifled as soon as they realize that, despite their energy and cooperation, they are unable to improve their performance and so unable to meet the requirements for a good grade. The interest of students in circuit training will be sustained much further when no evaluation is made.

Another form of evaluating fitness is enjoying increased popularity. All students who improve their average performance at the second maximum performance score test are given a coloured ribbon to be attached to their gym clothes. And all those who are successful in increasing their average scores at the second, more demanding, level of exercise (those in the "red circuit") are allowed to attach a second ribbon, and so on. The students who accomplish the maximum standard for the "red circuit" (third level of loading) are awarded a third ribbon to their outfit. These rewards have a significant influence on the motivation of the students.

Yet another method of evaluation is to take into account the individual differences in physical abilities of students. This type of evaluation most suits the nature of circuit training. The procedure is as follows: the results scored by students on the first maximum performance score test form the basis for any future evaluation, since any fitness improvements depend to a large extent on enthusiasm and willingness of students to perform in school training or exercise on their own at home. On the basis of test results the students are roughly divided into three categories, the very good, the average, and the poor category.

Category 1
Very good initial performance results. It is worth noting that high initial results cannot be improved upon as quickly as relatively lower ones. Therefore, for all students whose results in the first maximum test are at very high levels, the evaluations scheme shown in Table 28 may be used.

Category 2
Average initial performance. All students who scored somewhere around the average level may be evaluated on the basis of evaluation scheme presented in Table 29.

Category 3
Poor initial performance. For all students who scored around the mini-

Table 28   Evaluation scheme in school training.

Classification	Increase or Decrease of Reps. per Station	Total Change (10 exercises)
A	+3	+30
B	+2	+20 to +29
C	± 0 to +1	± 0 to +19
D	-1	-1 to -19
E	-2	from -20

Table 29   Evaluation scheme in school training.

Evaluation	Increase or Decrease of Reps. per Station	Total Change (10 exercises)
A	+4	+40
B	+3	+30 to +39
C	± 0 to +2	± 0 to -29
D	-2	-1 to -29
E	-3	from -30

mum level on the first maximum performance score test, the evaluation scheme in Table 30 is appropriate.

We consider these varying grade levels to be suitable for evaluating individual fitness improvement. Positive improvement should always be recognized with a higher grade. Experience shows that healthy students whose interest in exercising is about average always improve on their initial results. A drop in performance is usually observed only among those students who are unable to participate in class as a result of either long periods of absence (through illness, for example) or who show apparent unwillingness to exercise because of a lack of interest. Discipline problems may also be involved. Thus,

Table 30   Evaluation scheme in school training.

Evaluation	Increase or Decrease of Reps. per Station	Total Change (10 exercises)
A	+5	+50
B	+3	+30 to +49
C	± 0 to +2	± 0 to +29
D	-1	-1 to -19
E	-2	from -20

using our evaluation scheme as a guide, a physically weak student, for example, may justifiably be given an excellent mark after the second maximum test because he or she exercises conscientiously at home as well as in class, whereas another student who, in spite of absolutely better results, shows a lack of enthusiasm for the exercises, may be awarded a poorer mark. Although we recommend it unequivocally, the evaluation scheme outlined above should be used as guide; instructors are encouraged to modify its components according to their own needs.

12 Anatomical Classification of Circuit Training Exercises

All circuit exercises presented in this book have been classified into six major categories,as follows:

Category I: Exercises to develop the leg muscles
1. Squats: (a) both legs (b) single leg
2. Stepping exercises
3. Hopping, leaping and jumping exercises, with or without apparatus

Category II: Exercises to develop the arm and shoulder muscles
1. Pressing exercises - extending movements
2. Heaving exercises - flexing movements
3. Gripping exercises - holding and wrist rolling movements

Category III: Exercise to develop the abdominal muscles
1. The trunk moves towards the fixed legs
2. The legs move towards the fixed trunk
3. The trunk and legs move towards each other
4. Barbell exercises

Category IV: Exercise to develop the back muscles
1. Trunk lifts with legs fixed
2. Leg curls with trunk fixed

Category V: Combined exercises

Category VI: Partner exercises
1. For leg muscles

2. For arm and shoulder muscles
3. For trunk and abdominal muscles
4. *For trunk and back muscles*

I.   Exercises to Develop the Leg Muscles

The numbers in brackets refer to the illustrations shown in the next
section, pp. 135-161.

1a. *Squats using both legs*
• quarter squat   - knee joint forms an angle of 120° (1)
• half squat   - knee joint forms an angle of 90° (2)
• deep squat   - knee joint forms an angle of 30° (3-4)
    - with or without additional load, such as:
        medicine ball (2)   barbell (8 a,b)
        horizontal bar (5 a, b) weighted jacket
        dumbbell (6 a-c)   partner (9 a, b)
        sandbag (7 a-c)
    - with or without transferring weight onto toes (5 b, 8 b).

1b. *Single-leg squats*
• on the floor, with or without support (10 a, b; 11 a, b); with or with-
    out additional load (12 a, b; 13 a, b)
• on apparatus: - chair (14 a, b)
    - long bench (15 a-c)
    - with or without additional load (14, 15)

2. *Stepping exercises*
• stepping on with left leg, following with right leg; stepping off back-
    ward with left leg, and so on.
    - on long bench (16 a, b)
    - on box
    - with or without additional load, such as:
        medicine ball   dumbbells (17 a, b)
        sandbag   weighted jacket
        barbell   partner
• stepping on with left leg, stepping off with right leg, half turn;
• stepping on with right leg, stepping off with left leg, half turn, and
    so on, on box

- with or without additional load (18 a-f)

3. *Hopping and jumping exercises*
- hopping without apparatus, using both legs (19), using one leg (20) on the spot, forward, and sideways.
  - with or without snatching both knees, or the knee of the take-off leg up to the chest
- stretch jumps
  - with or without squatting (19, 20)
  - with or without additional load (23)
- jumps on apparatus or over obstacles
- stretch jumps
  - using both legs, using one leg
  - forward and sideways, with or without squats over a chain of medicine balls (24; 25 a, b), sections of boxes, hurdles, with or without intermediate hop (26)
- star jumps, using both legs, forward, as above (27)
- stretch jumps and squat jumps
  - with or without additional load, such as:
    | dumbbells | sandbag behind neck (28 a, b) |
    | round weights | weighted jacket |
- box jumps
  - from stand or squat stand
  - with or without additional load (30, 31)
- jumps over the long bench
  - continuous stretch jumps
  - sideways using both legs (32 a-c), or using one leg (33 a, b)
  - with or without squats (34 a-b)
  - with or without additional load, such as:
    | medicine ball | round weights |
    | sandbag | weighted jacket |
    | dumbbells | |
- single-leg stretch jumps
  - thrusting off the bench
  - with or without additional load (35 a, b)
- continuous squat jumps from legs astride position sideways (36)
  - legs astride position - with bench between legs
- bench jumps
  - on the spot and with forward movement (37 a, b)
  - with or without tucking knees into the chest

- with or without additional load (38 a-c) such as:
  dumbbells   sandbag behind neck
  round weights   weighted jacket
• hops and stretch jumps with skipping rope
  - from a standing position, with or without squats (39)
  - with skipping rope (41) and without skipping rope (40 a, b)
  - hopping in squat position
  - holding skipping rope in one hand and swinging it through under feet (42)
• squat jumps
  - with or without additional load (43 a, b), such as:
    sandbag behind neck   round weights shots
    barbell   weighted jacket
  - with or without simultaneous kicking out of both legs (43 b)
  - kicking legs alternately (cossack dance 44 a, b)
  - with or without partner (168 a, b)
  - barbell behind neck
  - transferring weight onto toes - with or without moderate or vigorous jump (22 a, b)
• star jumps on two boxes
  - with round weight, dumbbell, sandbag (45 a, b)
• duck walk (distance measured in metres)
  - with or without additional load (46 a, b), such as:
    medicine ball   barbell
    sandbag   weighted jacket

II.   Exercises to develop the arm and shoulder muscles

1. *Pressing exercises - extending movements*
• bending and extending of arms, i.e., push-ups
  - push-ups against wall (47 a-c), table, chair, gymnastic bench, or something similar (48 a, b)
  - push-ups from gymnastic bench, box or chair: thighs rest on an elevated support (49 a, b); lower legs rest on an elevated support (50 a, b); toes rest on an elevated support (51 a, b)
  - push-ups on the hands and on the finger tips (52 a, b, 53 a,) with additional, load such as:
    sandbag behind neck
    partner

- push-ups with clapping of hands, i.e., propelling hands and feet off the floor and clapping (54 a, b)
- push-ups as a partner exercise (173) with forward movement, stepping on and off a box, with additional weight (sandbag or weighed jacket) behind neck
- dips on the parallel bars at shoulder or full height
  - upward jump into support position at end of parallel bars, jump off with or without swinging (55 a, b, 59 a-d)
  - with additional load, such as:
    medicine ball between legs
    sandbag attached to legs
    weighted shoes
- chair dips (56)
- tuck dips (57)
- L-seat dips (58)
- press-ups
  - on the box, table or between two boxes (60 a, b)
- barbell jerk (61)
  - with horizontal bar or barbell, using one arm or both arms with split (61 b), or without split (63 a-c)
- standing press (62)
- one-armed clean and press (63)
- front press (64)
- military press (65)
- behind-the-neck press (66)
- bench press (67)
- dumbbell press (68)
- dumbbell bench press (69)
  - both arms simultaneously, or alternating left/right
- clean and press - kettle bell (70)
- seated clean and press - kettle bell (71)
- seated clean and press (72)
- chest expander (73)
- back expander (74)
  - using one or both arms

2. *Heaving exercises - arm bends or pulling with arms straight towards body or away from body*
   - with over-grip, under-grip, or mixed grip
- chin-ups gripping and holding movement

- with over-grip (77 a, b), under-grip (81 a, b), or mixed grip (84 a, b)
- on low horizontal bar, parallel bars, asymmetric bars, balance beam (78 a, b), table and on rings
- heels supported on floor or above shoulder height (77, 78, 81) with additional load, such as:
     weighted jacket
     sandbag (80, 83)
     partner (85)
- chin-ups - jump to grasp the bar
  - on the high bar (86 a, b), on the beam, on the ladder (87 a-c), on the rings; with additional load, such as:
       weighted jacket
       weighted shoes
- chin-ups from stretch hang
  - with over-grip (88 a, b), under-grip or mixed grip
  - on high bar, beam, rings, ladder, wall bars
  - with legs brought forward in horizontal-position with or without additional load, such as:
       sandbag (88 a, b)   weighted jacket
       medicine ball   weighted shoes
       barbells   partner
- arm jumps on the ladder (89 a-c)
- bend over rowing (90, 91)
- bench pull-ups (92)
- seated curls (93)
- straight arm pullovers (94)
- flies (95)
- expander exercises (96), in standing position with arms straight
  - from arms upward position to thighs
  - from arms upward sideways to hips
  - from arms sideways to chest
- heaving exercises with arms moving straight
  - from top to bottom (towards body)
  - from bottom to top (away from body)
  - sideways from top to bottom (towards body)
  - sideways from bottom to shoulder level
  - from sideways to front of body
  - from front of body sideways to arms spread sideways
These and similar exercises may also be performed using wall pul-

leys, expander and similar apparatus while standing, sitting and in supine position.
• arm-lifting exercises with dumbbell or barbell
  - with over-grip and under-grip in standing or seating position

3. *Gripping exercises for holding and wrist rolling movement*
All heaving exercises serve also as gripping exercises. The type of grip (over-grip, under-grip or mixed grip) is immaterial. Climbing, swinging on the horizontal bar, on the rings, on the rope or hanging bar can be labelled gripping exercises. Hands can greatly strengthened through wrist rolling exercise.

Barbell exercises always require a firm grip. No related examples have been given here; the anatomical classification of the barbell exercises receives attention elsewhere (see pp. 156 and 157).

III.   Exercises to develop the abdominal muscles

1. *The trunk moves towards the fixed legs*
• sit-ups from supine position
  - to seated position, forehead touches knee (97 a-c)
  - with or without additional load, such as:
    medicine ball   barbell discs
    sandbag   weighted jacket
• sit-ups with legs fixed
  - feet under wall bars (98 a-c)
  - at overturned long bench
  - on parallel bars
  - under cupboard
• Roman chair sit-ups (99)
  - twisting (100, 103)
  - on box with partner (101)
  - with or without additional load, such as:
    sandbag   medicine ball (102)
    weighted jacket
    barbell disc

2. *The legs move towards the fixed trunk.*
    The trunk is fixed under wall bars, bench, or by partner.
• raising and lowering of legs in supine position

These exercises strengthen straight abdominal muscles.
- up to a right angle with body - beyond right angle position with or
  without additional load, such as:
     medicine ball   sandbag
     weighted shoes
- on the floor,on the box (104 a-c), on an inclined bench
- raising both legs - simultaneously and alternately
- with weighted shoes or sandbag
• in supine position, performing double leg and figure-eight rotations.
  These exercises strengthen oblique abdominal muscles.
  - the trunk is fixed by holding onto the wall bars, bench, cupboard,
    partner
  - with or without additional load, such as:
       medicine ball
       weighted shoes
  - performing figure eight alternately to the left and right
  - bringing left toe to right ear, right toe to left ear alternately
• raising and lowering of legs from stretch hang
  - on wall bars, ladder, horizontal bar, on the rings, rope, climbing
    pole, high bar
  - legs bent (105 a-d) or legs stretched
  - up to horizontal position (106 a, b)
  - beyond horizontal position (108)
  - with or without additional load, such as:
       medicine ball (105 d, 107, 109)
       sandbag
       weighted shoes
  - open and close legs in horizontal position at wall bars (110 a-c)
• double-leg or figure-eight rotations in stretch hang for strengthening
  oblique abdominal muscles and iliopsoas
  - on wall bars (111 a, b) on horizontal bar, on rings
  - with or without additional load, such as:
       medicine ball   weighted shoes
• pulling up and over
  - on low horizontal bar (with over-grip, under-grip or mixed grip),
    climbing pole, rope (148 a, b) and high bar
• pulling up with half turn (as in pole vaulting)
  - without bar held in front, feet raised on a box or similar support
  - over bar of lower level to same height or higher (gripping height)

- dead lift with back straight (129, 30)
- dead lift with expander (131)
- twisted trunk curls
- seated on the box or weightlifters bench (132 a-d)
  - standing (133 a-d)
  - with additional load, such as:
      iron bar   round weight
      horizontal bar   medicine ball
      barbell
- straddle lift (134 a, b)

2. *Leg lifts with trunk fixed*
- raising and lowering legs from inverted stretch hang
  - on wall bars (135 a-c)
  - end of parallel bars (136 a-d)
  - also on rings, climbing pole, high bar with or without additional load, such as:
      medicine ball   sandbag
      weighted shoes
- hip extension or leg curls - raising and lowering legs in prone position
  - on the floor (137 a, b)
  - on box (138 a, b)
  - with or without additional load, such as:
      medicine ball (139 a, b) sandbag
      weighted shoes   elastic rope (bicycle inner tube)
- raising and lowering legs to free support scale
  - on the table, box, parallel bars (140 a, b)

V.   Combined exercise

- squat thrusts
- without push-up (141 a-c)
  - without stretch jump, yielding easily from ankles only
  - without push-up - with vigorous stretch jump
  - with push-up and bringing legs to chest (142 a-c)
- squatting and pressing with bench (143 a-c)
- climbs with legs crossed
  - on pole, rope (144), two poles

3. *The trunk and legs move towards each other.*
   These exercises strengthen straight and oblique abdominal muscles and iliopsoas.
- sitting tucks
  - squatting and stretching (112 a, b)
  - opening and closing of legs (113 a, c)
  - opening and crossing legs over (114), also over a medicine ball
  - raising and lowering straight legs, alternating (115 a, b)
  - from left to right and alternating over a medicine ball (116 a-c)
  - "cycling" (117 a, b)
  - from supine position lifting trunk to sit-up position, sliding the hands along the thighs as far as possible (118 a, b)
  - "jack-knife" (119 a, b)
  - sitting up and squat stand (120 a-c)

4. *Barbell exercises*
- barbell swinging
  - with over-grip (121 a-c)
  - under-grip (122 a-c)

IV.   Exercises to develop the back muscles

1. *Trunk lifts with legs fixed*
   These exercises involve lifting and lowering trunk in standing and prone position.
- trunk lifts
  - on the floor
  - on the long bench (123 a, b; 124 a, b)
  - on the box (125, 126)
  - on the parallel bars (127 a, b)
  - legs fixed under wall bars or held by partner
  - with or without additional load, such as:
      holding medicine ball with both hands
      sandbag behind neck
      weighted jacket
- standing-trunk curls forward (note: back must be held straight!)
  - with or without light additional load behind neck, such as:
      medicine ball   sandbag (128 a, b)
      horizontal bar   barbell

- rope ladder climbs (145)
- climbing with arms only
  - with or without legs held forward, or with weighted shoes, medicine ball
  - on climbing pole, rope (146), rope ladder (147)
- pulling up and over
  - on the rope, hanging bar, climbing pole (148 a, b)
- rope swings
  - without chin-up pushing off with feet (149 a, b)
  - with chin-up, without pushing off (150 a, b)
  - with medicine ball between feet (151)
- tuck dips on parallel bars at shoulder height
  - jumping into support position, with legs in squat position
  - "pumping" with legs held in horizontal position
  - medicine ball between legs (153 a, b)
- sandbag or hammer swings
  - using both arms (154 a-c)
  - using one arm (155 a, b)
- barbell exercises
  - clean and press (156 a-e)
  - snatch with squat technique (157)
  - full clean and jerk (159 a-e)
  - standing snatch (160 a-d)
  - with or without split technique, with squat when replacing barbell
  - squat jerk (161 a-c)
  - split jerk (162 a, b)
  - forward jerk to a 3-count-rhythm
  - jerking the barbell forward and upward with legs astride or alternating split technique (163)
  - barbell swings
  - arms bent with over-grip or under-grip (165 a, b)
  - arms straight with over-grip (164 a-c) or under-grip (166)

VI.   Partner exercises

1. *Exercises to strengthen leg muscles*
- leaping over partner (167 a-d)
- cossack dance (168 a, b)
- partner half-squats (169)

- bell ringing on wall ladder (170)
- leaning tower (171)
- medicine ball leaning tower (172)

2. *Exercises to strengthen arm and shoulder muscles*
- partner push-ups on box top (173 a-c)
- double push-ups (174, 175, 177)
- piggyback push-ups (176)
- dead man lifts (178)
- partner pull-ups (179)
- partner pull-ups on balance beam (180)
- wrestling drills
  - neck fight (181)
  - tug fight using one arm (182)
  - tug fight using both arms (183)
  - wrist fight - forcing partner into knee position (184)

3. *Exercises to strengthen trunk and abdominal muscles*
- wrestling with partner back-to-back with legs astride (185 a, b)
- supported sit-ups from supine position (186)
  - partner straightens legs from squat position
- leg raises with partner (187)
  - combined with partner raising and lowering trunk in supine position (187 c-d)
- trunk twists (188 a)
- trunk curls (189, 190, 191)

4. *Exercises to strengthen trunk and back muscles*
- trunk extensions
  - on the floor in prone position (193 a,b)
  - partner-supported (194)
- body lifters (195, 196)
- assisted trunk flexion with legs astride (197)
- arms locked trunk bends forward and backward (198)

Advice for the Execution of the Exercises

Frequent application and improper execution of certain body-building exercises, particularly when carried out in sets, may cause injuries to the young developing body, especially in the knee and lower back regions. For orthopedic reasons, then, certain exercises should not be undertaken in school programs at all, or else the following instructions should be adhered to:

• When performing knee bending exercises and jumps (particularly with additional load), the angle of the knee joint should not, if possible, exceed 90° (see Figures 4, 5 a, 5 c, 7 c, 23 b, 27 b, 31 a).

• Lifting of an additional load while standing, and trunk bending forward (see Figures 90 and 91, 129 and others) should be replaced by the exercises described in Fig. 92.

• In performing exercises described in Figures 90 and 91, athletes must keep their backs straight.

• In exercises such as in Figures 123 b, 124 b, 126 b, 128 b, 129, the trunk should be lifted only slightly beyond the horizontal position.

• When doing standing dumbbell swings as a combined exercise, such as in Figure 164, the trunk should be bent forward only slightly for gathering momentum, with the back kept straight.

Circuit training exercises are illustrated on pages 136 to 162.

15a 15b 15c 16a 16b

17a 17b 18a 18b 18c

18d 18e 18 19a 19b 20a 20b

21a 21b 22a 22b 23a 23b 24

25a   25b   26a   26b

27a   27b   27c   28a   28b

29a   29b   29c   29d

30a   30b   30c   31a   31b

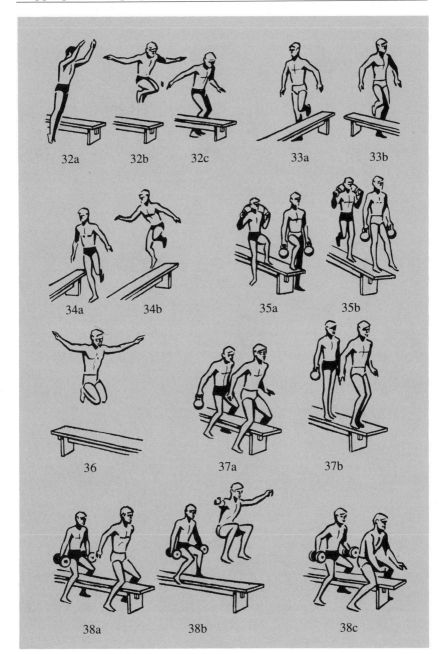

32a 32b 32c 33a 33b

34a 34b 35a 35b

36 37a 37b

38a 38b 38c

39

40a   40b   41   42

43a   43b   44a   44b

45a   45b   46a   46b

47a   47b   47c

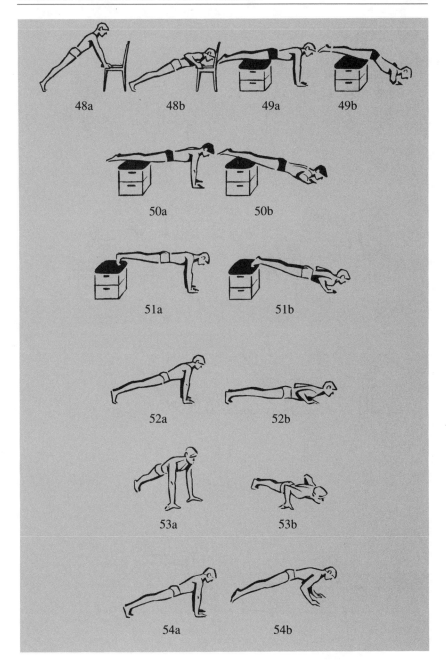

48a 48b 49a 49b

50a 50b

51a 51b

52a 52b

53a 53b

54a 54b

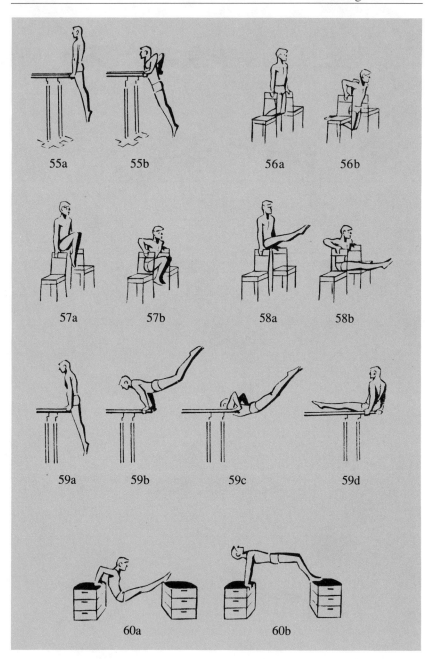

55a   55b   56a   56b

57a   57b   58a   58b

59a   59b   59c   59d

60a   60b

61a 61b 62a 62b

63a 63b 63c

64a 64b 65a 65b 66a 66b

67b 67a 68a 68b

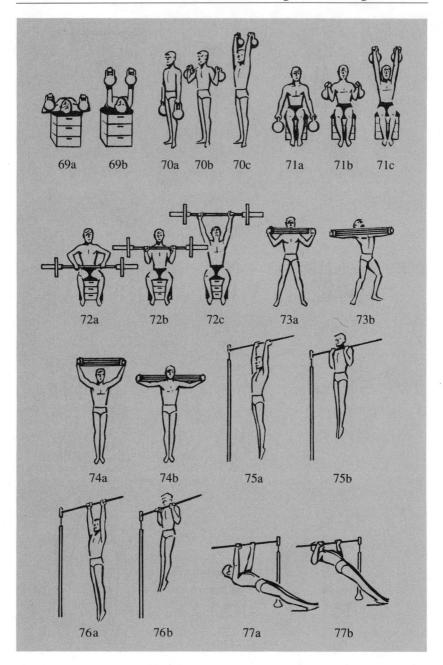

69a   69b   70a   70b   70c   71a   71b   71c

72a   72b   72c   73a   73b

74a   74b   75a   75b

76a   76b   77a   77b

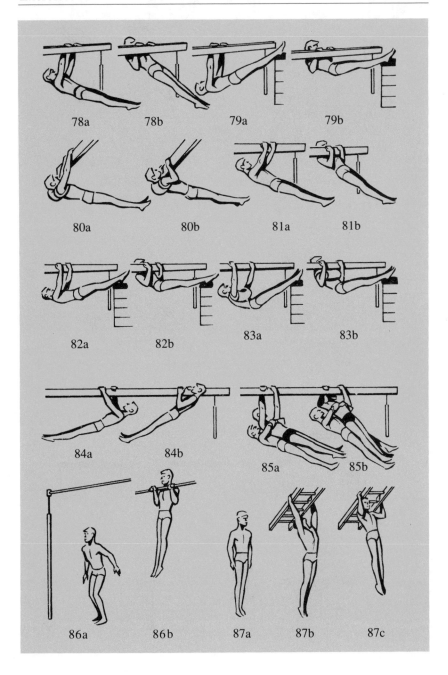

78a 78b 79a 79b

80a 80b 81a 81b

82a 82b 83a 83b

84a 84b 85a 85b

86a 86b 87a 87b 87c

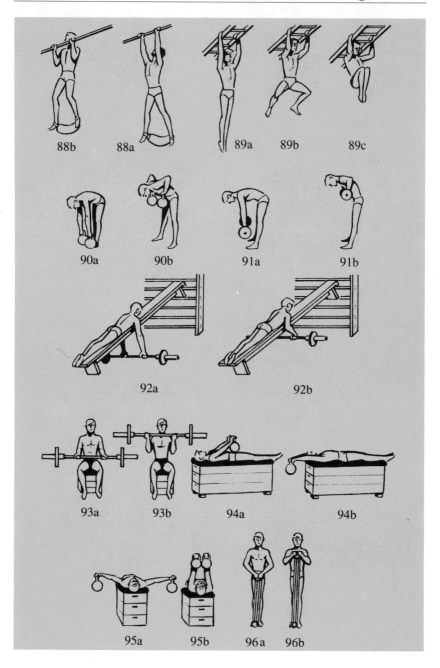

88b   88a   89a   89b   89c

90a   90b   91a   91b

92a   92b

93a   93b   94a   94b

95a   95b   96a   96b

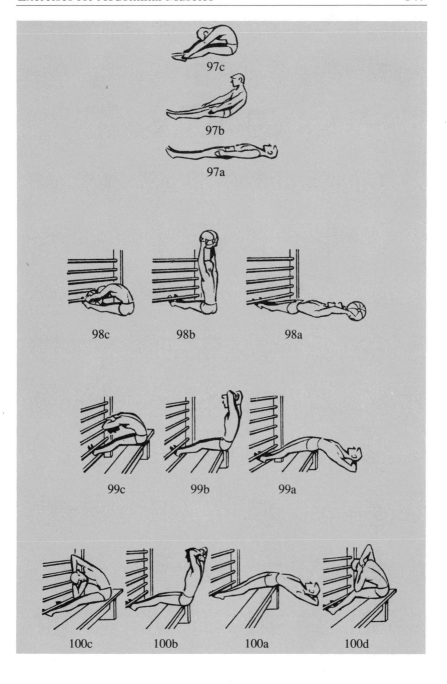

97c

97b

97a

98c   98b   98a

99c   99b   99a

100c   100b   100a   100d

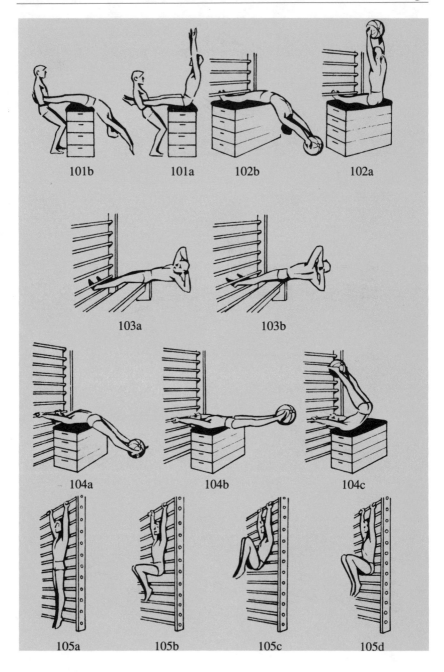

101b   101a   102b   102a

103a   103b

104a   104b   104c

105a   105b   105c   105d

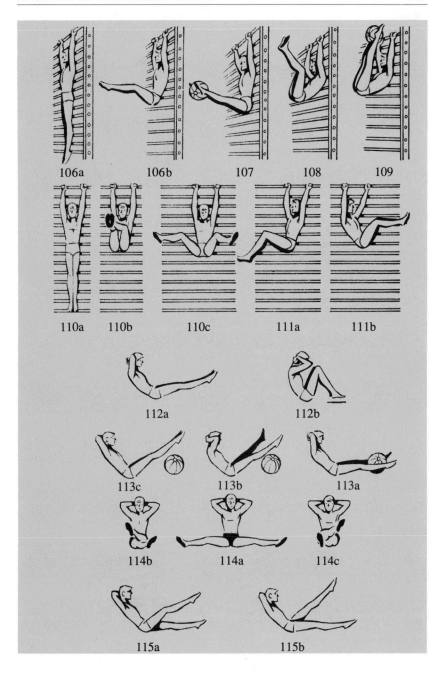

106a 106b 107 108 109

110a 110b 110c 111a 111b

112a 112b

113c 113b 113a

114b 114a 114c

115a 115b

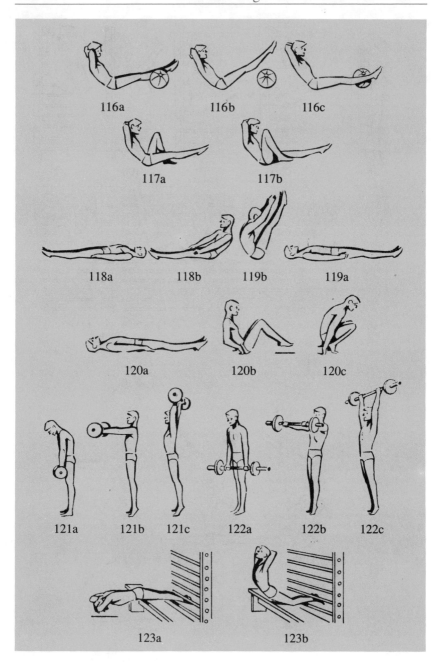

116a   116b   116c

117a   117b

118a   118b   119b   119a

120a   120b   120c

121a   121b   121c   122a   122b   122c

123a   123b

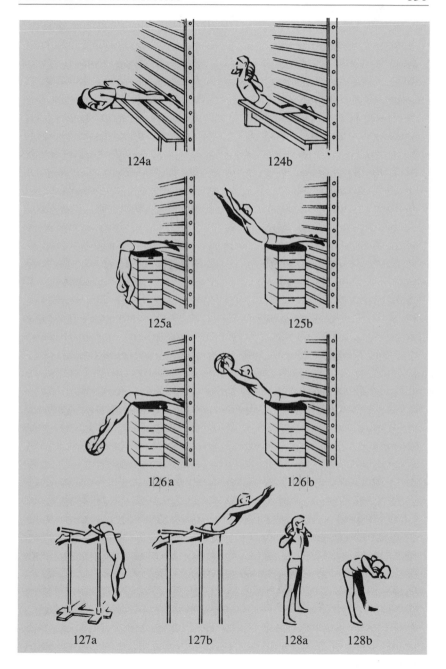

124a   124b

125a   125b

126a   126b

127a   127b   128a   128b

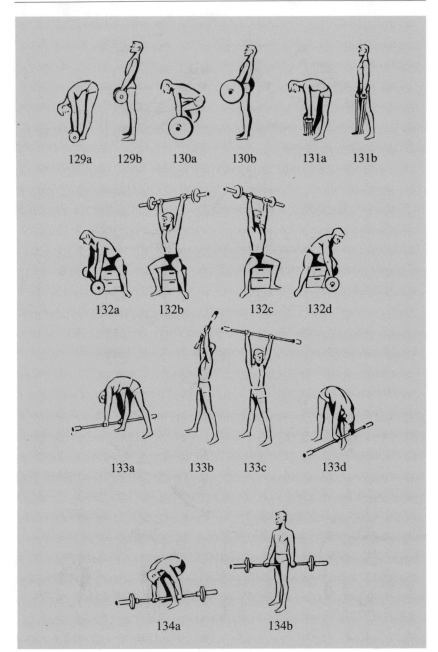

129a   129b   130a   130b   131a   131b

132a   132b   132c   132d

133a   133b   133c   133d

134a   134b

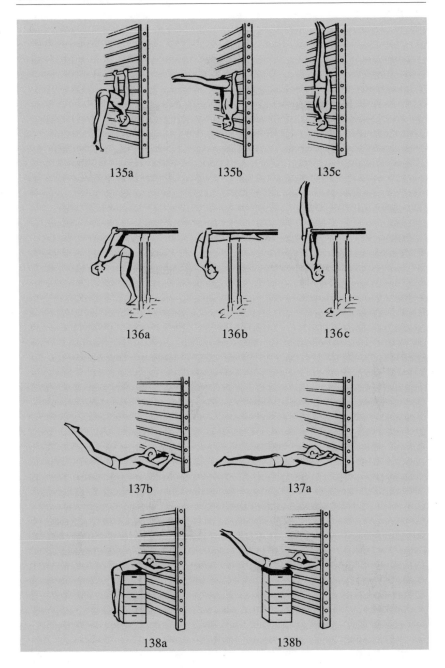

135a 135b 135c

136a 136b 136c

137b 137a

138a 138b

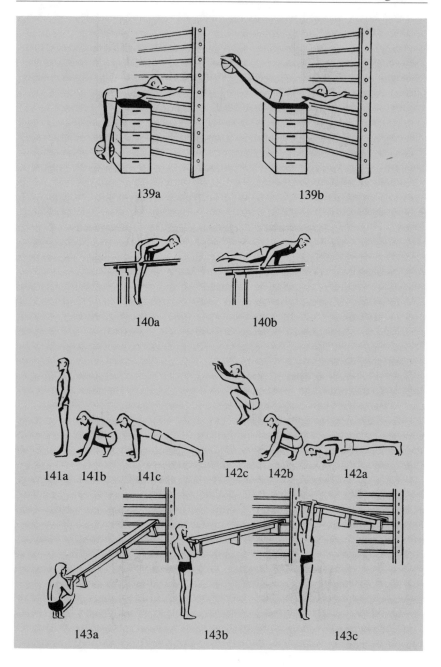

139a   139b

140a   140b

141a   141b   141c   142c   142b   142a

143a   143b   143c

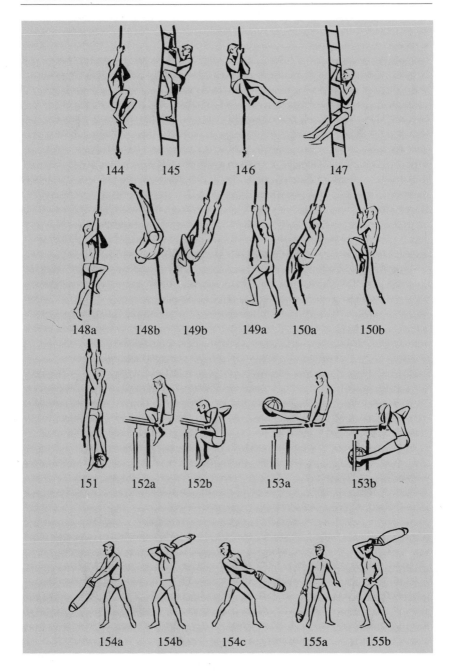

144   145   146   147

148a   148b   149b   149a   150a   150b

151   152a   152b   153a   153b

154a   154b   154c   155a   155b

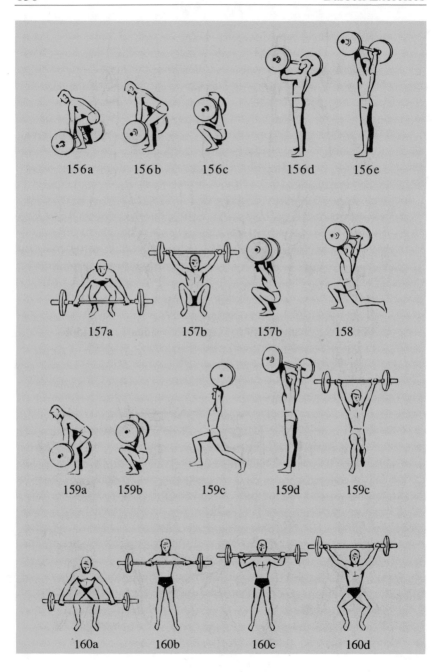

156a   156b   156c   156d   156e

157a   157b   157b   158

159a   159b   159c   159d   159c

160a   160b   160c   160d

161a 161 161b 162a 162b

163 164a 164b 164c

165b 165a 166a 166b 166c

VI

167a 167b 167c 167d

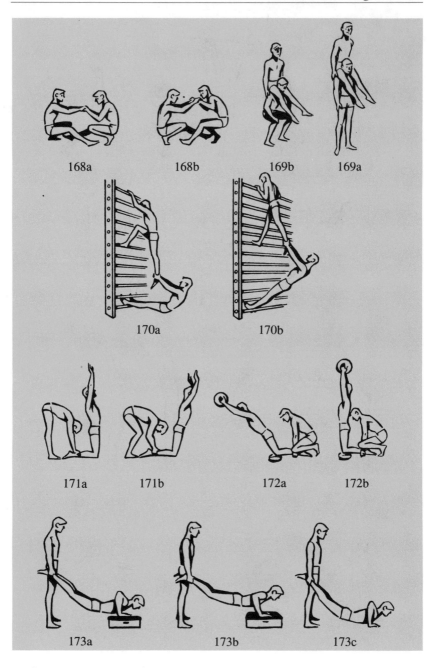

168a   168b   169b   169a

170a   170b

171a   171b   172a   172b

173a   173b   173c

174a

174b

175a

175b

176a

176b

176c

177a

177b

177c

177d

178a

178b

178d

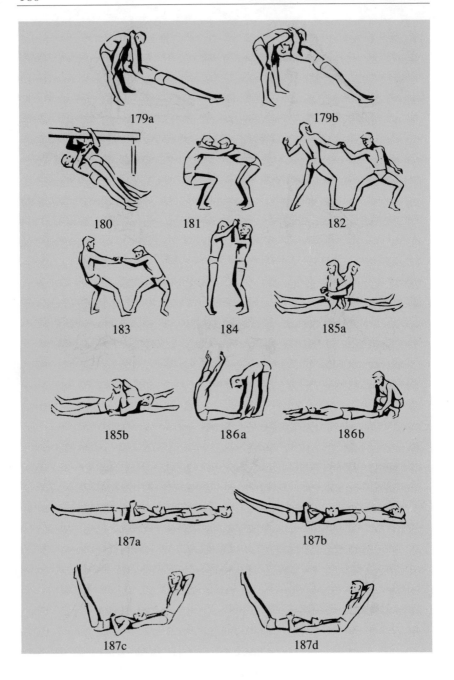

179a

179b

180

181

182

183

184

185a

185b

186a

186b

187a

187b

187c

187d

188a
188b

189a
189b
190a
190b

191a
191b
192a
192b

193a
193b

194a
194b

195a

195b

196a

196b

197a

197b

198a

198b

198c

The examples of general and specific circuit training programs are presented in the next chapter.

13 Examples of General and Specific Circuit Trainings Programs

Exercising by stations in school programs for the 9-10 age group in preparation for circuit work and circuit training

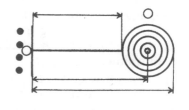

4 stations; exercising time 5 min; 8 students per station;
• 1 min rest period for changing station

Station 1 **Performance test**
1 x 60 m run or 2 x 30 m
• 3 runners, 1 starter, 2 timekeepers

Station 2 **Throwing at target**
• with hard ball/club 3 x 3 throws

Station 3 **Long jump**
• continuous activity
• with 5-step run-up
• leaping from box top
• distance marker

Station 4 **Medicine ball throws**
5 repetitions per exercise
3-4 laps
E1 Two-handed passes
• with both hands from chest
• from astride/step position
• elbows at shoulder height
E2 Putting or throwing
• alternating right and left
• from frontal step position
E3 Throwing towards partner
• from bent trunk position forward
Changing sides (for all students)

Exercising by stations in school programs for the 9-10 age group in preparation for circuit work and circuit training

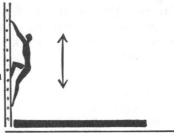

Example: various apparatus; work over an obstacle course; warming up 5 min; exercises at 6 stations each involving 4-6 students; exercising for 30 min; pursuit race 5 min; clearing apparatus away 5 min

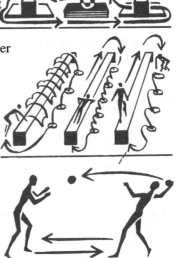

Station 1 **Wall bars and mat**
climbing up and down

Station 2 **2 box sections and 1 box top**
• crawling under - jumping over - crawling under
• slalom race
• crawling under - forward roll - jumping over

Station 3 **2 long benches and 5 gymnastic hoops**
• zig-zag jumps (one way)
  - single leg hops (return)
• pulling along bench in prone position (one way)
  - bunny hops (return)
• tiptoeing with arms stretched out (one way) - frog hops (return)

Station 4 **Gymnastic balls**
• passing ball (one-handed)
  - catching ball (two-handed)
• as above, with partners changing sides

Station 5 **Parallel bars; 1 bar - 3 students**
• jumping into support position
• chin in balance suppor tposition
• inverted squat hang from balance support hang

Station 6 Box, balance beam, mat

- balancing on balance beam (with aid of partner)
- jumping down onto mat and forward roll
- piggyback (return)

Ending lesson with team pursuit race
(the apparatus remains in place
for the next group of students)
- dose: 3 x 1 lap per group
- starting sequence:

1st lap group	2nd lap group	3rd lap group
1:2	1:3	1:4
3:4	2:5	2:6
5:6	4:6	3:5

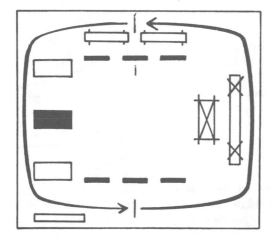

Circuit work in shool progams and basic training for the 9-10 age group in preparation for circuit training

E1 Alternating squat jumps
- over long bench
- on the spot
- with slight forward movement

E2 Sit-ups
- from supine position and
  trunk curls forward/down
  to fixed legs
- with additional load
- without additional load

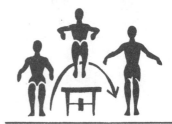

E3 Jumping sideways
- over long bench

E4 Rotated grasp swings
- on wall bars/bench or box
- without additional load
- with additional load

E5 Jumping to support position
- on parallel bars (end of bars) at chest
  or shoulder height - jumping down

E6 Figure-eight rotations
- with medicine ball through straddled
  legs

E7 Skipping
- on the spot

E8 Leg lifts
- from hanging position
- knees to chin
- instep kicking

E9 Squat thrusts
- with/without stretch jump

E10 Reverse curls
- from supine position to point of grasp
  of hands
- with straight or bent legs

**Circuit work in school programs
for the 9-10 age group in preparation
for circuit training: basic training**

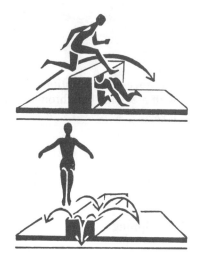

E1 Jumping over and crawling through
- section of boxes

E2 Continuous side jumps
- into and out of open section of boxes

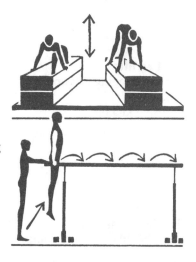

E3 Jumping into crouch support position
- from a standing position in box

E4 Jumping into support and pressing
- at end of parallel bars
• jumping down
  jumping into seated position,
  legs astride
• jumping into support and pressing
  jumping down and running to

  end of parallel bars, moving
  forward on hands (approximately
  for the 13-14 plus age group)

E5 Rolling
- on box top
• forward
• backward

E6 Swinging into handstand
- against wall

E7 Flying straddle jumps
- with intermediate hop

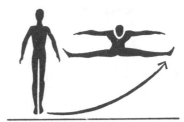

E8 Cartwheels
- continuously
- alternating left/right hand

E9 Squatting through
- on pommelled horse to rear support

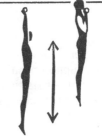

E10 Chin-ups
- after jumping to the horizontal bar
- with over-grip/under grip

Circuit work in school programs for the 11-12 age group: basic training using gymnastics exercises

E1 Raising into upstart hang
- rolling through into inverted hang
- backward movement
- from standing position
- from stretch hang
- variations of leg posture

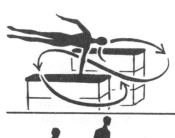

E2 Side vault/front vault/squat vault
- over two boxes,
- alternating left/right

E3 Straddle vault
- over chain of bucks from a 3-step run-up - forward roll

E4 Jumping and pressing into support
- on horizontal bar (chest height)
- hip circle forward through kip hang into stretch hang

E5 Free hip swing
- into front support position
- from stepping or starting position on horizontal bar (chest/stretch height)
- jumping down

E6 Forward roll
- from squatting/standing position
  into squatting/standing/sitting
  position, followed by backward roll and
  into squatting/standing position
- with flying handstand
- using handstand, or
- with stretch in handstand and half turn

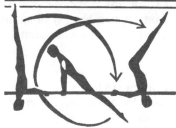

E7 Inverted kip
- on horizontal bar continuously

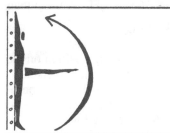

E8 Leg raises
- from a hanging position into horizontal
  position - opening and closing of legs

E9 Lifting into headstand
- from squat/straddle stand/
  press-up position
- also rolling forward - stretch
  jump with half turn, or pressing
  into handstand

E10 Chin-ups
- on the high bar with
  over-grip or under-grip
- with take-off
- from stretch hang
- with/without additional load

**Intensive interval circuit work with
varying loads in school programs for
the 10-11 and 15-16 age groups (with or
without additional load)**
3 students exercise at each station
consecutively

E1 Chin-ups
- from support hang with inclined balance
- 15-16 year olds with sandbag upon chest

E2 Sideways leaps
- from the ankles over overturned long
  bench
- 15-16 year olds with sandbag on back

E3 Trunk curls
- forward/backward
  in front riding position on the
  long bench with legs fixed
- (head touches the mat when
  bending backward and the bench
  when bending forward)
- 15-16 year olds with medicine ball

E4 Squat thrusts
- without/with stretch jumps
- without/with bending of arms
- 15-16 year olds with stretch jump

E5 Jumping jack
- with medicine ball
- 15-16 year olds with 20-30 kg barbell

E6 Sit-ups
- from supine position to squat stand and stand
- 15-16 year olds with stretch jump

E7 Jumping over and crawling through
- sections of box
- 15-16 year olds over 76-cm hurdle

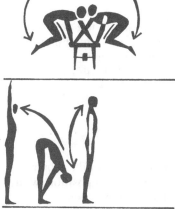

E8 Alternating squat jumps
- over the long bench/low box

E9 Trunk bends forward
- in starting position
- in straddle position
- 15-16 year olds with barbell

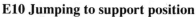

E10 Jumping to support position
- at end of parallel bars (chest height) jumping down
- 15-16 year olds on high parallel bars, or with dips

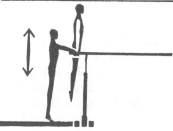

Intensive interval circuit work in school programs forthe 12-13 age group: basic training

E1 Step jumping
- from a 3-5 step run-up
- jumping off right/left from box top
- loading on the leading leg
- continuous running

  6 x (3 x left / 3 x right)

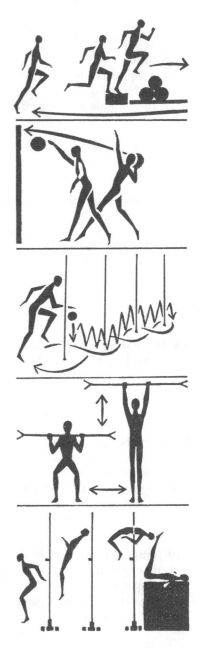

E2 Puttingm a medicine ball
against the wall
• from a frontal position
• from a putting position
  10 x (5 x right / 5 x left)
- stretch both ankles
- elbows are behind the ball
- fingers point towards chin

E3 Ball dribbling and slalom course
- around 4 to 6 high jump
  stands/javelins
- with basketball/handball
- 5 x

E4 Jerking
- horizontal bar/dumbbell
- from starting position, with
  knees slightly bent
  from the chest

E5 High jumps
- forward squat jumps with a
  3-step run-up,
- or standing Fosbury flop
  over stretched rubber band
  inclined to horizontal, or over
  pole secured with rubber band
  as controlled jumps onto pile of mats

E6 Medicine ball throws
- with both hands and arched back
- against the wall
  with legs slightly astride/
  stepping position
- right-handed students using left
  leg before right
- 10 x

E7 Combination
- push-ups immediately followed
  by star jumps
- 3 x 3 combined exercises

E8 Hard ball throws
- against the wall
- from basic position advance left
  leg to stepping position
- with hard ball/handball
- also target throws
- 10 x

E9 One-legged jumps over long bench
- slight forward movement
  with/without additional load
- 6 x (alternating left/right)

E10 Jack-knife
- with straddled legs
- clapping hands on the floor
- 10 x

Intensive interval circuit work/circuit training for accentuating the arm and trunk muscles

E1 Medicine ball throws
- against the wall
- from supine position to sit-up position (legs are fixed!)

E2 Medicine ball throws
- backward over the head towards the wall
- from forward-bend position

E3 Chin-ups
• from balance support
  with inclined hang
  with/without additional load
  (sandbag), or
• from take-off to the high
  horizontal bar/ladder

E4 Sandbag swinging
- two-handed/one-handed circles
  as in hammer throwing
- bottom of swing at bottom
  right, top of swing at top left)
- grip with right hand
  over left hand

E5 Squat thrusts
• without stretch jump
• with stretch jump

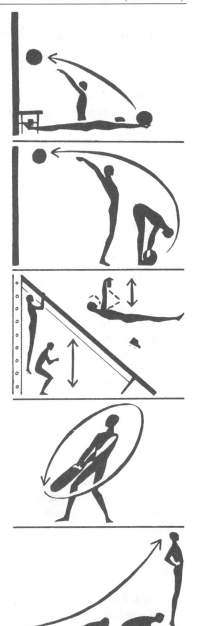

E6 Rebound throws
- with hard ball/medicine ball
  against the wall
- from frontal position/throwing
  position
- left/right

E7 Squat and press with bench
- from a standing position
  (chest height) with slightly bent knees
- from a deep squat position
- under-grip

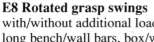

E8 Rotated grasp swings
with/without additional load
long bench/wall bars, box/wall
bars, box/parallel bars

E9 Arm jumps, or hanging walk
- on horizontal/inclined ladder/beam

E10 Pulling up and over
- on rope/swing/high parallel bars
  with mixed grip

Intensive interval circuit training

E1 Chin-ups
- in balance support with inclined hang
  on balance beam/horizontal bar

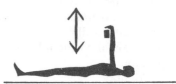

E2 Duck walk
- measured in metres

E3 Jack-knife

E4 Push-ups
• usual way
• with hand-clapping

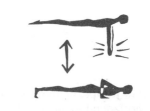

E5 Simultaneous trunk and leg raises
- from prone position
- also as chopping knife
  exercise

E6 Press-ups reverse
- between 2 boxes
- with arching of hips

E7 Star jumps
- with squatting and
  hands between legs

E8 Sit-ups
- from supine position
  into squat stand

E9 Medicine ball throws
- two-handed
  against the wall
  from astride/stepping position

E10 Leg raises
- from supine position

Intensive and extensive interval circuit training

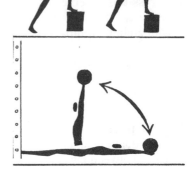

E1 Stepping on and off
- long bench/box
- also with jump-down
- alternating left/right

E2 Sit-ups
from supine position
- also with medicine ball

E3 Push-ups
- without hand-clapping
- with hand-clapping

E4 Stretch jumps
- from ankles
  over medicine ball and bench
- forward and backward
- sideways

E5 Rotated grasp swings
- without medicine ball
- with medicine ball
- on box/bench - on wall bars

E6 Squats
- • stretching ankles
- • with slight take-off
- - with/without additional load

E7 Leg raises
- - from a hanging position or
  raising of legs to horizontal position

E8 Rebound throws against the wall
- - with legs slightly astride or in
  stepping position
- - elbows at shoulder height

E9 Squat thrusts
- - with stretch jump

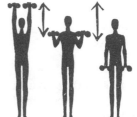

E10 Cleaning and jerking 2 dumbbells

Intensive circuit training for accentuating leg muscles

E1 Stretch jumps
- from half squat
- with slight forward movement gently absorbing momentum on the balls of the feet

E2 Push-ups
- with hand-clapping

E3 Deep squats
- with slight take-off stretching of the ankles
- without additional load
- with sandbag 5-7.5 kg

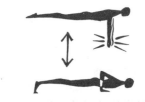

E4 Jack-knife
- with legs astride and hand-clapping on the floor

E5 Alternating thrusts
- using split technique left/right
- with/without turn

E6 Sit ups
- from supine position to squat stand

E7 "Cherbakis"
- left/right or matching thigh thrusts
• on the spot
• with slight forward movement

E8 Leg raises
- from hanging position

E9 High throwing of medicine ball
- from a relaxed trunk curl
- forward position and with legs
  slightly astride

E10 Squat thrusts
- bending arms and with stretch jump

Intensive interval circuit training for accentuating the leg muscles in sprinters, runners, jumpers
(performing relaxing exercise after work at each station, e.g. E1 + E1a; 2 + E2a; etc.)

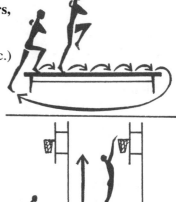

E1 One-legged hops
- on the long bench;
  6 x left / 6 x right
- with/without additional load

E2 Stretch jumps
- with the knees slightly bent
- touching the basketball board/basket
- with both hands
- using a height marker

E3 Kicking out the legs
- from a squat position
• flat
• with progressive height gain

E4 "Cherbakis"
• with/without thrusting out
  lower leg
• on the spot - with/without
  alternating of legs
• with slight forward
  movement and 6 alternating
  the legs

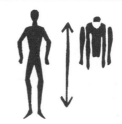

E5 Star jumps
- with knees apart
- arms between legs

E1a Tensing and relaxing

- in supine position - tucking in the legs and clasping arms tightly round the legs; tense to the count of 5
- supine position - legs slightly astride, feet slightly turned outward (so-called "ten -to-two" position), arms lying flat on the floor alongside body with palms pointing upward

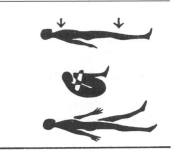

E2a Tensing and relaxing

- in prone position - lifting trunk, arms and legs; remaining tensed to the count of 5
- resting head, arms (apart), legs (astride) on floor

E3a Tensing and relaxing

- in supine position - arms and legs pressed against the floor to the count of 5
- shoulder stand with arm support - cycling and shaking out legs sideways

E4a Tensing and relaxing

- in supine position while resting on arms
- raising legs, stretching feet, opening and closing legs to the count of 5

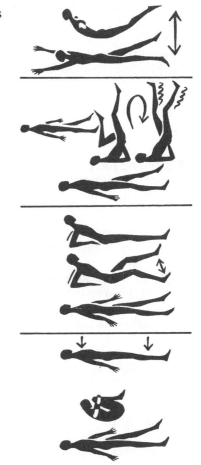

E5a Tensing and relaxing

- in supine position - as in 1a

E6 Alternating hops
- with/without "yielding"
  in squat support, right/left
  with leg undercuts, sideways,
  right/left

E7 Stretch jumps
- with rapid hip twist, or
- into arched tension and
  "twisting" both legs and head
  round to the right/left
- looking over shoulder down to heels

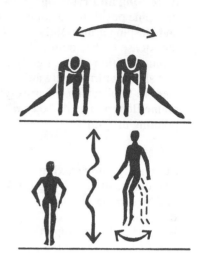

E8 Running jumps
without/over obstacles
2 x up to 3 x 20 m

E9 Stretch jumps
- with knees slightly bent
- on the spot
- with slight forward movement
- coming down on the balls of the
  feet
- with additional load (sandbag)

E10 Push-ups
- with hand-clapping and striking
  feet together (propulsion from floor)

E6a Tensing and relaxing

- in supine position and resting
  on forearms - flat and slow
  cycling with tensed muscles to the
  count of 5
- placing feet down on floor
  with legs bent, then shaking
  out vigorously

E7a Tensing and relaxing

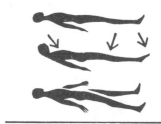

- in supine position with chin resting on
  chest; arms, hands and legs pressed
  against the floor to the count of 5
- resting head on floor with
  mouth slightly open and turning
  palms upward, feet at
  "ten-to-two" position"

E8a Tensing and relaxing

- in angle support seat;
  raising tensed legs as high as
  possible while sitting up
- resting legs on floor slightly
  astride with feet at
  "ten-to-two-position", then
  shaking out legs

E9a Tensing and relaxing

- in prone position, stretching
  out arms with whole body
  pressed against the floor to the
  count of 5
- changing to supine position
- relaxing as in E7a

E10a Tensing and relaxing

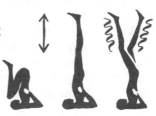

- in supine position, tucking legs to the
  chest, clasping arms around legs, raising
  knees to the chest to the count of 5
- shoulder stand with support of arms -
  kicking both legs simultaneously
  upwards in a relaxed manner, then
  shaking out legs

"Short circuits" for home training

Easy "short circuit"
E1 inclined balance support
E2 trunk curls in seated position stretched
E3 flying splits, yielding easily
E4 raising trunk to horizontal position -
    bending forward with legs astride

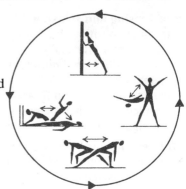

Intermediate "short circuit"
E1 press-up
E2 jack-knife exercises
E3 deep knee bends
E4 trunk bending and stretching with legs
    astride (head between legs)

Difficult "short circuit"
E1 push-up with the feet
      resting on an elevated support
E2 angle sitting
        a) opening and closing legs
        b) squatting and stretching legs
        c) crossing legs
E3 one-legged knee bends
E4 in starting position, bending
      trunk and twisting trunk (with
      each stretch, legs are kicked
      backward alternating left and
      right leg)

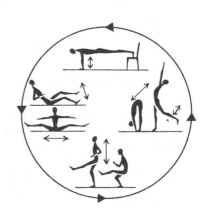

14 Improving Sport-Specific Performance Through Circuit Training

In order to apply circuit training programs for particular sports the following principles must be taken into account:

• Circuit training programs with general exercises form the basis for sport-specific programs.

• Sport-specific circuit training programs for particular sports may consist of:
  - exercises for developing general and specific abilities;
  - exercises for developing specific abilities;
  - exercises for developing specific abilities, with relaxing or limbering-up exercises and/or stretching exercises.

• The dynamic structure for developing specific abilities corresponds wholly or partially to that of competition exercises. Thus, the following exercises are suitable for particular sports- or events-specific circuit training programs:
  - specific preparatory exercises;
  - basic exercises;
  - exercises intended for improving a specific ability.
  These exercises have a clearly defined starting and ending position. They can also be repeated cyclically despite an acyclic sequence. They involve a relatively low degree of technical complexity.

• For sports-specific circuit training programs, maximum tests are generally not necessary. Coaches decide upon training levels on the basis of students' age, sex, and fitness levels, as well as their training experiences. The number of repetitions is determined on the basis of those repetitions at relative intensity levels that are reasonable and/or essential for meeting the set training goals.

Taking into account the demands made by training practice, we

Table 31   An overview of sport-specific use of circuit training methods.

Category of sports	Aim to be achieved	Structure of circuit training method
endurance sports	• endurance	- endurance method; - extensive interval method;
	• strength endurance	- extensive inteval method; - endurance method;
	• power	- intensive interval method:
	• power plus endurance repetitions;	- with/without time limit; - with/without set no. of
sports requiring strength and power	• maximal strength	- repetitions method - pyramid system; - set no. of repetitions and of additional load per set;
	• power	- repetition method - set no. of repetitions; - exercising against the clock;
	• power plus endurance	- intensive interval method - with/without time limit, with/without set no. of repetitions, extended interval;
	• strength - endurance	- extensive and intensive interval method with/without time limit, with/without quota of repetitions;
	• aerobic endurance	- extensive interval method; endurance method.

have put together a list of examples of sports- or events-specific circuit training programs that can be used for a variety of sports. From the numerous sports-specific training exercises we have chosen ten whose effectiveness has been proven for putting a circuit training program together. It is our hope that coaches and athletes will be encouraged to use these exercises in an even more creative manner. They are intended to serve merely as a guide for choosing the most appropriate exercises to be used in training.

The goal of training in every kind of sports is to develop those abilities that are most important for competitive fitness and to maintain these abilities and skills at a high level. When using a sports- or discipline-specific circuit training program, therefore, any goal-oriented development of fitness-specific skills is dependent not only on those exercises selected on the basis of their movement structure, but also on the way in which that program is organized and implemented using a particular circuit training method. Because the ultimate aim is to improve sport-specific performance systematically, which may be specific or general but always positive, the basic concept of circuit training structure involves a number of variations as shown in Table 31.

14.1   Examples of Sports Specific Circuit Training Programs

I. Athletics (track and field)

1. Sprint, middle-, long-distance
2. Hurdles, steeplechase
3. Walking
4. Long jump and triple jump
5. High jump, roll
6. High jump, flop
7. Pole vaulting
8. Shot putting
9. Discus throwing
10. Hammer throwing
11. Javelin throwing

II. Ball games

1. Volleyball
2. Handball
3. Basketball
4. Volleyball

III. Winter sports

1. Speed skating
2. Cross-country skiing
3. Combined downhill/slalom competition
4. Ski-jumping

IV. Swimming

V. Rowing

VI. Cycling

VII. Single combat sports

1. Boxing
2. Wrestling
3. Judo

VIII. Apparatus gymnastics

IX. Strength sports

I.1 Circuit training for running: endurance, intensive, and extensive interval method

E1 Walking with knees lifted
- short steps with high frequency
- arms and legs move in harmony

E2 Push-ups
- with hand-clapping and striking feet together

E3 Jack-knife
- with straddled legs
- clapping hands on floor

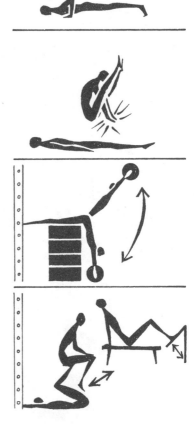

E4 Trunk lifts
- on box and wall bars with additional load, such as sandbag, medicine ball

E5 Leg extensions
- on leg press apparatus, or from supine position pressing upward and with locked legs pushing partner off

E6 Chin-ups
- from support hang with inclined balance, stretch hang
- on horizontal bar, on balance beam
- jumping up to high bar, ladder, beam (also climbing with arms only)

E7 Squat thrusts
- with stretch jump
- with push-ups, stretch jump, and squatting

E8 Figure eight rotations with legs
- stretched hang of wall bars or high bar/and circling legs
- over height marker

E9 Star jumps
- over obstacles (5 hurdles, 76-100 cm high/box sections/ medicine balls), 1 m to 2.5 m apart
- with/without intermediate hops

E10 Thigh curls
- in prone position

I.2 Circuit training for hurdles and steeple chase: intensive and extensive interval methods

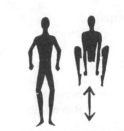

E1 Star jumps
- arms between legs
- with intermediate hops
- without intermediate hops

E2 Hurdling
- with one stride between hurdles (3-4 m apart)
- without stride between hurdles (1.5-2.5 m apart), height of hurdles 40-100 cm

E3 Jack-knife
- with hands clapping the floor between straddled legs

E4 Push-ups
- with hand-clapping and feet striking together

E5 Step jumping
- over a hurdle, forward and backward
(e.g., swinging over with left leg/pulling through with right leg - forward;returning left leg/returning right leg, etc.)

E6 "Cherbakis"
- kicking lower leg forward and upward
- on the spot one-legged left/right
- with slight forward movement, alternating legs

E7 Hurdle seat
- from hurdle seat with left leg forward into hurdle seat with right leg forward via press-up roll or
- changing support from hurdle seat left (left leg forward) to right leg

E8 Medicine ball throws
- from deep trunk curl forward backward over head against the wall
- turning - catching - turning back to starting position

E9 Alternating hops
- with extremely high kicks (left/right)
- clapping hands under the knee of the kicking leg
- start kick with leg sharply bent

E10 Medicine ball throws
- against the wall from supine position
- with fixed straddled legs

I.3 Circuit training for walking: endurance and extensive interval method$_s$

E1 Duck walk
measured in metres

E2 Swinging trunk rotations with medicine ball
- in slightly straddles position
  swinging out loosely 1 x left, then
  proceeding immediately to
  trunk rotation, right

E3 Squat thrusts
- do not bend and stretch arms
- with stretch jump

E4 Double leg circles on the rings
- left and right, if possible
  (otherwise performer's best side)

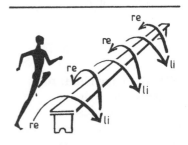

E5 Cross jumps
- over long bench

E6 Alternating jack-knife and push-ups
- changing from supine to prone
  position and vice versa

E7 Frog jumps
- flat forward jumps from full squat
  position
- landing on arms first

E8 Sandbag swinging
- to the left and to the right

E9 Stretch jumps
- with hip twist

E10 Chopping knife

I.4 Circuit training for long and triple jumps: intensive interval method

E1 Jumping off and on
- using two boxes (height 40-80 cm, 1-2 m apart)
- without additional load

E2 Medicine ball throws
- against the wall or up into the air aiming for height
- from low trunk curl forward
- with slight take-off for throwing

E3 Alternating thrusts
- leaping using split technique
• without turn
• with turn

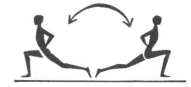

E4 Arching the pelvis
- in supine position with head and feet resting on an elevated support

E5 "Cherbakis"
• between two boxes, or
• on the spot, one-sided left/right
• with slight forward movement alternating left/right

E6 Alternating jack-knife and push-ups
- with propulsion
  from floor

E7 Jumping
- with 3- or 5-count rhythm
- from mat to mat
- over medicine balls
- from a standing or
  starting-off position
  lift thighs as high as possible

E8 Medicine ball throws
- against the wall
  from supine position
  with legs fixed

E9 Take-offs
- with/without light additional load
- on the long bench with slight
  forward movement
  or
- on the spot using the box

E10 Sandbag swinging

I.5 Circuit training for high jump (roll): intensive interval method
- without time limit;
  6-10 repetitions; 60-sec pause

E1 One leg take-offs from the ankle using both arms
- swinging leg is loosely stretched on box
- light additional load possible

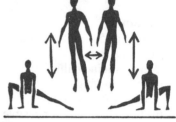

E2 Leg thrusts
- from squat press-up position and split technique sideways, from left to right

E3 Stretched forward and upward swings
- with left/right leg
- from press-up position
- from supine position on inclined bench
- standing in front of box/wall bars
- toes pointing towards shin

E4 Hopping from pike position
- flat
- with progressive gain of height

E5 Stepping jumps
- starting with a 3-5 step run-up
- to bar placed above jumping height
- jumping onto table

E6 Stretch jumps
- starting with knees slightly bent
  with additional load
  or
- from deep squat between two boxes
  and holding round weight with both
  hands

E7 Hurdle seat
- changing support from left to
  right and pressing forward
  resiliently with forehead towards knee

E8 High jump squats
- over 5-6 hurdles
- landing on jumping leg

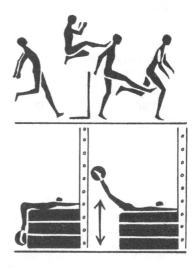

E9 Leg curls
- from prone position on box -
  with hands holding wall bars
- with or without medicine ball
  between legs

E10 Squat jumps
- over 5 hurdles
  80-100 cm apart height of
  60-100 cm
  After landing on balls of feet
  prepare for immediate
  take-off! Clean squat position
  above hurdle!

I.6 Circuit training for high jump (flop): intensive interval method
without time limit; 6-10 repetitions; 60-sec pause

E1 Trunk curls
- forward and backward
  with feet slightly astride
- finger tips touching toes and
  heels

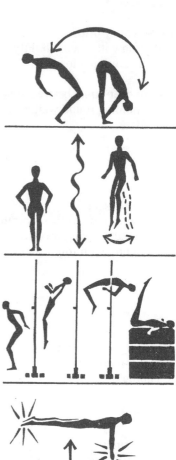

E2 Stretch jumps
- with hip twists
  on the spot

E3 Standing flop
- over rubber band, or bar
  secured with rubber band
- landing on back on pile of
  mats with arms stretched out

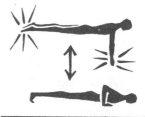

E4 Push-ups
- with clapping hands and striking
  feet together

E5 Jack-knife
- with straddled legs and
  clapping hands on the floor

E6 Stepping jumps
- into sitting position on vaulting table
- from a 3-5 step run-up

E7 Zig-zag jumps
- over long bench

E8 Touch jumps
- to the basketball board with a quarter turn
- take-off from one leg - touching with matching arm of the jumping leg, from inside to outside
- two-legged take-off and touching as above

E9 Forward and backward roll
- forward roll to standing position, springing up and turning
- backward roll through handstand to standing, and so forth

E10 Walking with hops
   aiming for height
- with accentuated swinging of leg to centre of body
- alternating left/right to enable a slight zig-zag course

I.7 Circuit training for pole vaulting: intensive and extensive interval methods

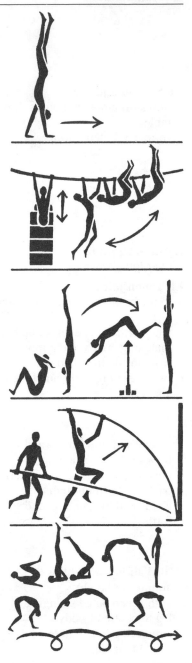

E1 Handstand walking

E2 Chin-ups in inverted stretch hang ("L" position)
- with mixed grip on the
  fixed fibre glass bar
  (horizontal) or parallel bar
- with/without legs touching floor

E3 Backward roll
- through handstand
  over bar

E4 Pole bending
- vigorously bending of pole
  against the wall
- from a 3-step run-up

E5 Floor springs
• neck springs
• headstand springs

E6 Leg lifts
- on wall bars, triangle, rope
• without additional lead
• with additional load

E7 Leg thrusts
- on the long bench/box
- alternating left/right leg
• without additional load
• with additional load

E8 Changing grip
• on fixed pole with left
  underarm support slight but
  noticeable bending of pole, or
• on rope, with/without leg
  support on box/table

E9 Hand springs
- sideways with quarter turn to
  land (half Arabian cartwheel)

E10 Climbing
- in inverted stretch hang or "I"
  position
- on climbing pole, rope

I.8 Circuit training for shot putting: intensive interval method

E1 Medicine ball throws
- against the wall
  using both hands
  from astride/stepping position
- elbows kept at shoulder height

E2 Jumping jack
- with barbell

E3 Straightening up
- from deep split position
  pressing up over heel
  with sandbag on shoulders
  (7-15 kg)

E4 Medicine ball throws
- against the wall
  from short approach (medicine
  ball lying on floor, picking up
  and approaching)

E5 Trunk bends sideways
- with additional load (sandbag,
  barbell)

E6 Medicine ball throws
- against the wall
  from putting position
- also from opposite stance
- important to stretch from both
  ankles

E7 Sit-ups
- from supine position on
  inclined long bench
- with additional load (sandbag)

E8 Alternating thrusts
- from flying split
  with additional load (sandbag)

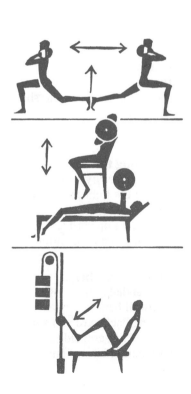

E9 Pressing the barbell
• from supine or seated position

E10 Leg extensions
• on the leg-press machine
• from supine position or
  straightening and bending legs
  on calf-machine, or
• from quarter squat stretching to
  toes and lifting slightly off the
  floor

I.9 Circuit training for discuss throwing: intensive interval method

E1 Rebound throws
- with medicine ball
  against the wall
- from a frontal position, with
  quarter and half turns

E2 Sit-ups with forward twists
- on bench/wall bars
- in straddled seat
- right elbow towards left knee
  and alternating
- without additional load
- with additional load

E3 Sandbag swings
using one arm
- also with round weight, short
  hammer

E4 Pressing the barbell
using 3-count **rhythm**
- jerking the light to medium-
  weight barbell off the chest,
  alternating upward and forward
  accompanied by position changes

E5 Trunk twist bends
- in extended sitting position on
  box/wall bars
- sinking backward and sideways
  to throwing-arm side
  with dumbbell, weight,
  iron bar

E6 Bench press
- from supine position
- with narrow/wide grip

E7 Swinging forward and backward
- two barbell discs
- lifting onto toes and swinging forward at same time

E8 Jumps
- onto box, and jumping off backwards
• without additional load
• with additional load

E9 Swinging trunk rotations
- with medicine ball
- in relaxed angle stand with legs astride

E10 Raising two discs
- from lateral position into position over chest
- from supine position on the bench

I.10 Circuit training for hammer throwing: intensive and extensive interval methods

E1 Leg lifts
- hanging on the wall bars swing-kicking each leg in turn to the point of grasp of the opposite hand

E2 Forward jumps
- with knees slightly bent and swinging barbell/medicine ball
- alternating left to right, while holding arms in front of chest
- axis of pelvis remains in frontal position

E3 Trunk twist bends
- from supine position with legs fixed
- both hands touching the floor beside the hips

E4 Cleaning the barbell
- narrow grip, straight back
- stretching legs to standing on toes

E5 Arm rotations
- with sandbag, two hammers, round weight

E6 Jerking the barbell
- from chest
- with change of stance

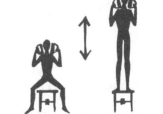

E7 Medicine ball throws
- two-handed rebound throwing against the wall
- starting position: back towards the wall medicine ball lying on right side behind right leg
- also alternating with left foot

E8 Jump-ups
- on the long bench from straddled position above bench
- with additional load

E9 Leg raises
- over medicine ball in "L" seat with counter-swinging of arms

E10 Trunk twist bends
- with barbell
- seated on bench

I.11 Circuit training for javelin throwing: intensive and extensive interval methods

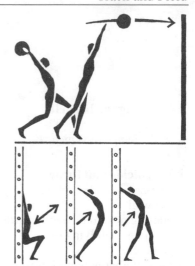

E1 Medicine ball throws
- against the wall
  two-handed from starting
  position into astride position,
- left leg in front of right for
  right-hand thrower

E2 Back arching
- from hanging squat stand
  on the wall bars
- both feet remaining at
  starting position or
- left leg is placed forward

E3 Combination exercise
- propulsion from floor
  fast turn and jack-knife

E4 Forward and backward swings of the arms
- in wide-angled straddle stance
  trunk is bent forward yielding
  slowly

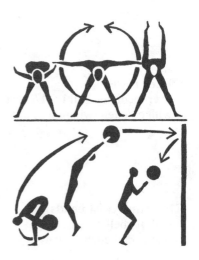

E5 Medicine ball throws
- backward over the head
- from extended forward trunk
  bend
- quick turn - catch, etc

E6 Alternating thrusts
- with extended split technique
  also with turn
- front leg forms an acute
  angle!

E7 Throws
- with hard ball against the wall
• from starting position
  placing left leg forward
  or
• from supine position

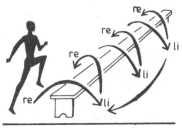

E8 Zig-zag jumps
- over long bench

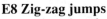

E9 Pullovers
- with barbell, round weight, shot
- from supine position on bench
- narrow grip, elbows parallel
  towards the front

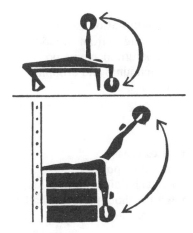

E10 Trunk lifts
• on box and wall bars
• with medicine ball

II.1 Circuit training for soccer: endurance, intensive, and extensive interval methods

E1 Distance jumps
- with head pushing towards height marker, such as suspended soccer-ball

E2 Throw-in
- with medicine ball against the wall
- from arched position and from slightly straddled or stepping stance

E3 Shooting
- against the wall with medicine ball
- alternating left/right
- the ball is pushed not kicked

E4 Combination exercise
- dropping to front support - quick turn to supine position - stretch jump and dropping forward, etc.

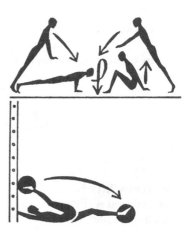

E5 Leg curls
- in supine position hands holding onto wall bars
• with/without medicine ball between legs

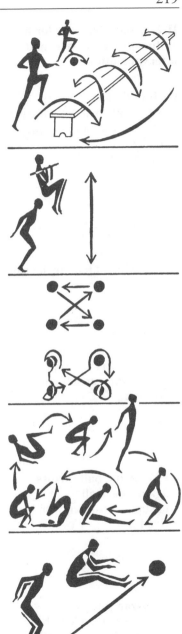

E6 Zig-zag leaps
- jumping sideways from left to right leg
- on the spot over medicine ball
- with forward movement over long bench

E7 Chin-ups
- jumping up to the high horizontal bar
- with legs squatted
- over-grip or under-grip

E8 Sprints
- with change of direction in a 5 x 5 m square
- left/right course
- with/without jumping over medicine ball (corner limit)

E9 Combination exercise
- dropping to supine position - swinging forward and up - stretch jump, and so forth
- also with backward roll

E10 Medicine ball
- pitching the ball with feet against the wall, from clasp hold or
- toes under the ball

II.2 Circuit training for handball: endurance, extensive, and intensive interval methods

E1 Ball throws
- with volleyball, light medicine ball, hollow ball
• against the wall
• into net or goal

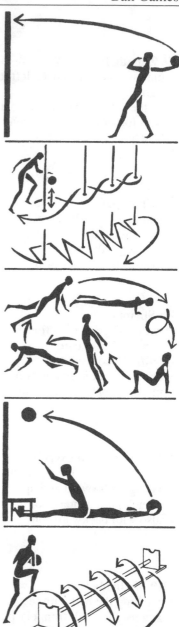

E2 Slalom course
• with ball dribbling
• without ball
- with/without feinting by side-stepping

E3 Combination exercise
- dropping to front support - quick turn - stretch jump, and so forth

E4 Medicine ball throws
- against the wall in supine position, with legs
- fixed

E5 Zig-zag jumps
- over overturned long bench
• without ball
• with ball dribbling

E6 Trunk lifts
- without trunk twists
- with trunk twists

E7 Sprints
- in a 5 x 5 m square
- without ball
- with ball dribbling
- with/without feinting

E8 Squat thrusts
- with stretch jump

E9 Jumping throws
- over height maker against the wall-
  retrieving the ball - running back
  to starting position

E10 Figure-**eight rotations**
- with medicine ball
  through straddled legs

II.3 Circuit training for basketball endurance, extensive, and intensive interval methods

E1 Sprints
- 5-6 m forward between two markers
- stopping - adjustment steps backward
- with/without ball

E2 Medicine ball throws
- against the wall
  from supine position, with legs
  fixed

E3 Touch jumps
- to basketball board/basket
- quick run-ups from mark at
  5-8 m distance
• also with ball and basket
  throws

E4 Figure-eight rotations
- with medicine ball
  through straddled legs

E5 Leaps
- over overturned long bench
  with/without ball dribbling
• hopping, left/right
• from left foot to right, from right to left
• zig-zag jumps
• two-legged jumps sideways,
  with/without intermediate hops

E6 Throwing basketball to the board (left/right)
- from the free-throw line
- moving in and catching the rebound and throwing into basket, etc

E7 Rebound throws
- with medicine ball against the wall

E8 Squat jumps
- over 5 hurdles/box sections
• with/without basketball
• with/without intermediate step and bouncing ball

E9 Propulsion from floor
- with quick turn from and back into prone position
- turning alternately to left and to right

E10 Stretch jumps
- touching basketball board/ basket
- with one hand or both hands
- without/with intermediate hop

II.4 Circuit training for volleyball: endurance, extensive, and intensive interval methods

E1 Japan test
- touching the side market
  (medicine ball)
- by hands
- by bum

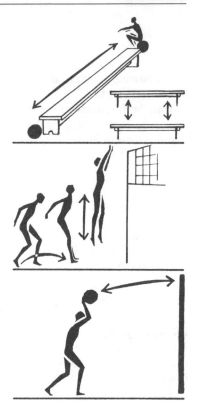

E2 Stretch jumps
- at the net to block (also at
  basketball board)
- with/without preliminary step
- take-off with both legs

E3 Rebound throws
- with medicine ball
  against the wall using height
  marker
- from a "tucked in" position

E4 Squat jumps
- over 5 hurdles/box sections
- with intermediate hops
- without intermediate hops

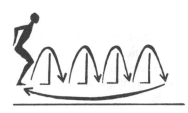

E5 From dredge position
- jumping into half-handstand
  rolling gently back over chest to
  dredge position, etc.

E6 Shuttle sprint
- 9-3-6-3-9 m shuttles
  forward and backward

E7 Medicine ball throws
- against the wall
  using both hands
  with arched back
- also throwing after stretch jump

E8 Extensive lateral splits to dredge position
- with adjustment steps
  between two marked lines
- with adjustment steps
  through under net

E9 Trunk lifts
- with trunk curls
  on box and wall bars

E10 Medicine ball throws
- forward and upward
  from low trunk bend
- without take-off
- with take-off

III.1 Circuit training for speed skating: endurance, extensive, and intensive interval methods

E1 Zig-zag jumps
- in normal/bent posture
- on the spot over medicine ball
- over long bench with forward movement
- also two-legged lateral jumps

E2 Trunk lifts
- on box and wall bars
- without additional load
- with additional load

E3 Frog jumps
- aiming for distance
- knees slightly bent with trunk bent forward and keeping arms behind back

E4 Chin-ups
- from inclined support hang or
- with take-off to high bar and squatting of legs

E5 Alternating step jumps
- from not higher than half squat
- without additional load
- with additional load

E6 Combination exercise
- changing from jack-knife to push-up
  position and vice versa

E7 Squats into jumping
- using one leg (other leg is
  held out in front)
- without/with holding onto
  wall bars or similar
- also cossack dance (forward/
  sideways)

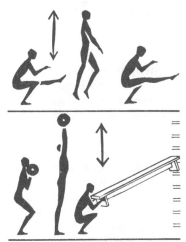

E8 Jumping jack
- with/without additional load
  or
- squatting and pressing with
  bench

E9 Jumps
- from one leg to the other
  also with arms kept behind the
  back
- in squatting front support
  position, visibly leaving the floor

E10 Simple stretch jumps
- with hip twist
  or
- hip twist without stretch
  jump

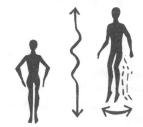

III.2 Circuit training for cross-country skiing: endurance, extensive, and intensive interval methods

E1 Pulling exercises
- alternating left/right
- using rubber band/expander on wall bars/pulley

E2 Stepping exercises
- on box or long bench
• without additional load
• with additional load

E3 Medicine ball throws
- against the wall
  through the straddled legs -
  quick turn - catch - back to
  starting position
- rising onto toes to get a wide swing

E4 Pressing with bench
- from squat position
  stretching until standing on toes to
  support the bench at full height
- slight take-off from the floor

E5 Jack-knife
- turning around longitudinal body
  axis (left/right) - jack-knife -
  turning, etc

E6 Zig-zag jumps
- over long bench
  jumping sideways from left to
  right, right to left, etc.
- on the spot
- with forward movement

E7 Trunk lifts
- on box and wall bars
- without trunk curls
- without additional load

E8 Pulling exercises
- using both arms simultaneously
- working in two stages: straight trunk
  and bent trunk

E9 Squat thrusts
- with stretch jump
- with/without bending and
  stretching of arms
- with/without squatting of legs
  during stretch jump

E10 Reverse push-ups
- high kicks, alternating left/
  right leg

III.3 Circuit training for slalom/downhill skiing: endurance, extensive, and intensive interval methods

E1 Zig-zag jumps
- on the spot over medicine ball
- with forward movement
  over long bench
- on ski trainer

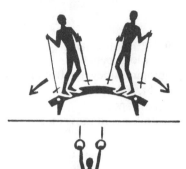

E2 Abdominal rotations
- on the rings

E3 Jumps
- in downhill racing posture
- with/without additional load
- on the spot
- with forward movement

E4 Slalom race
- as sprint only
- hip twist, counter position
- jumping onto leg outside arc

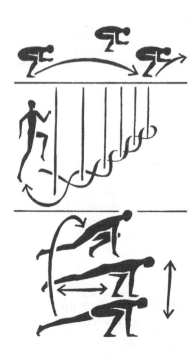

E5 Propulsion from floor
- from squatted front support
  left/right into squatted front support
  position right/left
- changing legs in mid-air

E6 Leg lifts

- hanging of the wall bars swing-kicking each leg in turn to the point of grasp of the opposite hand alternating left/right
- in supine position with hands fixed, left leg to right hand, and so forth

E7 Cossack dance

- also with body bent forward
- on the spot sideways
- with duck walk

E8 Combination exercise

- jack-knife - quick turns to left and right - propulsion from floor, and so forth

E9 Monkey jumps

- on wall bars

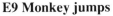

E10 Sandbag swings

- rotating left and right

III.4 Circuit training for ski-jumping: endurance, extensive, and intensive interval methods

E1 Alternating thrusts
- with flying split technique
- arms spread sideways in a relaxed manner
• with/without additional load

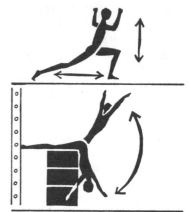

E2 Trunk lifts
- on box and wall bars
• with/without additional load

E3 Squat thrusts
- with stretch jumps and swinging arms backward and up

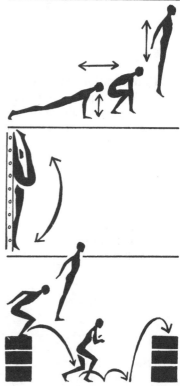

E4 Leg lifts
- from hanging of the wall bars
• without additional load
• with additional load

E5 Low leaps
- from box (50-100 cm) into telemark position
- after quick adjustment step jumping onto box - turning - jumping

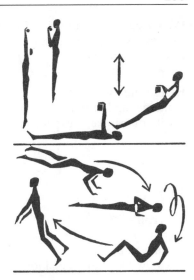

E6 Chin-ups
- from balance support hang
- from stretch hang

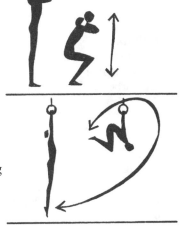

E7 Combination exercise
- dropping into push-up position-
  quick turn into supine position -
  squatting - supine position -
  dropping into push-up position, etc

E8 Squats
- without additional load
- with additional load

E9 Swinging on rings
- swing into inverted start -up and rolling
  back
- from stretch hang on
  rings/bar/parallel bars

E10 Sandbag swings
- to the left and right

IV. Circuit training for swimming: endurance, extensive, and intensive interval methods

E1 Pulling exercises
- alternating left/right
- with rubber band, expander, pulley

E2 Trunk lifts
- on long bench and wall bars/box and wall bars
• with/without additional load

E3 Pull-ups
- in prone position on inclined bench
- with barbell or horizontal bar

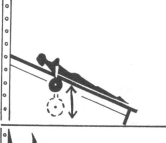

E4 Leg lifts
• hanging on wall bars or horizontal bar
• raising legs to horizontal position only

E5 Pulling exercises
- with both arms simultaneously
• standing
• lying

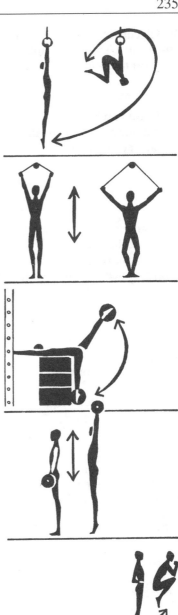

E6 Swinging on rings
- swing into inverted upstart position and rolling back
- from stretch hang on rings, parallel bars or horizontal bar

E7 Pulling exercises
- with both arms simultaneously from overhead to side position
- standing facing front then back
- lying prone/supine

E8 Hip extension
- from prone position on box and wall bars
- with/without additional load
- right/left leg alternating

E9 Barbell curls and press
- in standing position with light barbell or horizontal bar

E10 Squat thrusts
- with stretch jump
- with/without bending and stretching of arms
- with/without squatting of legs

V. Circuit training for rowing: endurance, extensive, and intensive interval methods

E1 Land rowing
- on home trainer or rowing
  machine/ergometer

E2 Medicine ball throws
- against the wall
  backward over head - quick
  turn - catching - throwing, etc

E3 Jerking the barbell
- from the chest
  from slight knee bend

E4 Leg curls
- in supine position
  with hands fixed
- with medicine ball between
  feet
- without additional weight

E5 Cleaning and replacing the barbell
- with straight back

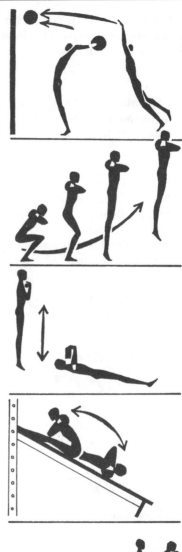

E6 Medicine ball throws
- from arched back stance
- against the wall

E7 Squats
- with sandbag
• without stretch jump
• with stretch jump

E8 Chin-ups
• in balance support with
  inclined hang
• from stretch hang
• with/without take-off
• with/without additional load

E9 Sit-ups and trunk bends forward
- from supine position on inclined
  bench
• with/without additional load

E10 Squat thrusts
- with stretch jump
• with/without bending and
  stretching of arms
• with/without squatting of
  legs

VI. Circuit training for cycling: endurance, extensive, and intensive interval methods

E1 Sprints
- on the home trainer
- maximum frequency

E2 Squat thrusts
- with stretch jump
• with/without bending and
  stretching of arms

E3 Squats
- with slight take-off
- from half squat
- with sandbag

E4 Jack-knife

E5 Stepping exercises
- on long bench or box
• without additional weight
• with sandbag (7.5-15 kg)

E6 Push-ups
- usual way/on finger tips/
  with hand-clapping
- with/without additional weight

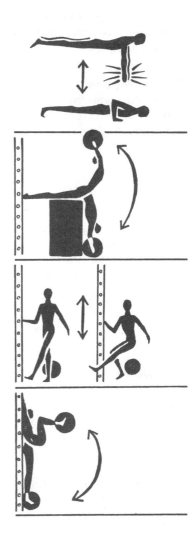

E7 Trunk lifts
- on box and wall bars
- with/without additional
  weight
- with/without trunk twists

E8 Squats
- using one leg
- with/without hand support
- briefly sitting on the
  medicine ball

**E9 Leg lifts from stretch hang
on wall bars**
- both legs simultaneously
  without/with additional load
- both legs alternately

E10 Duck walk
- measured in metres
- without additional load
- with additional load

VII.1 Circuit training for boxing: endurance, extensive, and intensive interval methods

E1 Medicine ball thrusts
- against the wall from boxing stance
- alternating left/right
- left/right only with maximum frequency

E2 Forward thrusts
- with dumbbell
- alternating legs

E3 Skipping
- with/without squats

E4 Quick trunk twists
- in straddled sitting position,
- clapping both hands on floor
- legs remaining fixed

E5 Punching
- straight/uppercuts, hooks to the side on punching bag or padded wall

E6 Jumping on and off gymnastic bench
- from straddled position
- without additional load
- with additional load

E7 Combination exercise
- push-up with hand-clapping -
  turning into supine position -
  jack-knife

E8 One-hand rebound throws
- with medicine ball against the
  wall
- with legs slightly astride
- frontal position
- backward position
- left and right only
- alternating left/right

E9 Uppercuts
- with dumbbell
  alternating left/right
  in boxing stance

E10 Boxing thrusts
- with raised trunk
  in prone position and
  legs fixed

VII.2 Circuit training for wrestling: endurance, extensive, and intensive interval methods

E1 Squat turns
- over long bench
- on the spot
- in forward movement

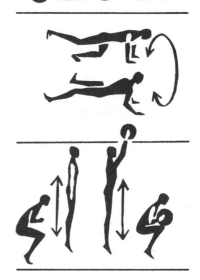

E2 Jack-knife
- if possible with medicine ball

E3 Leg undercuts
- sideways (undercutting) in front support position
- alternating left/right

E4 Star jumps
- with/without vertical thrusting of medicine ball to a height marker
- starting from and returning into deep squat

E5 Bridge rotations
- to the left/right
- alternating left/right

E6 Squat thrusts
- without stretch jump
- without push-ups

E7 Walkover
- from a standing position
  into bridge and fast walkover
  alternating left/right

E8 Bridge roll
- forward from knee stand returning
  into knee stand

E9 Trunk rotations
- with medicine ball
  in straddled angle stance
- alternating right/left

E10 Forward walkover
- forward/backward
  via headstand
- swing both legs simultaneously

VII.3 Circuit training for judo: endurance, extensive, and intensive interval methods

E1 Knee bends
- with partner
  in kata-guruma posture

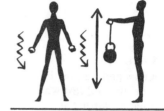

E2 Gripping exercise
- with/without tennis balls or
  grip squeezers also wrist rolling

E3 Lifting up partner
- partner in kesa-gatame posture
  via bridge

E4 Lifting partner off his feet and placing him down
- with/without throwing partner down
- uchi-komi-geiko
- using uki-goshi

E5 Leg undercuts
- in front support position alternating
  left/right (undercutting)
- fast and with swing

E6 Chin-ups
- in supine position/balance support hang on partner
- partner in straddled angle stance, with hand supported on knees

E7 Jack-knife
- with legs relaxed

E8 Propulsion from floor
- push-ups with hand-clapping and striking feet together over rolling partner - alternating

E9 Full sit-ups
- with firm hold around partner's waist

E10 Pulling
- with two rubber bands or expanders
- snatching from frontal combat stance and quick turn to left/ right

VIII. Circuit training for apparatus gymnastics: intensive and extensive interval methods

E1 Straight arm support swings on parallel bars
- with maximum amplitude of swing
- forward or backward swinging
- forward and backward swinging

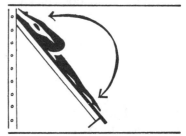

E2 Quick leg raises
- on inclined bench and wall bars
  (also as whip-like movement of
  legs, followed by opening of the
  arm/trunk and leg/trunk angles)

E3 Bending forward and backward
- on the box and bar, or box and
  hand bars

E4 Opening of the arm/trunk angle
- quick and vigorous action
  at the rolling board and wall
  bars - with ring ropes
  in prone position - head down

E5 Stretch jumps
- over sections of boxes (3-5)
  followed by jumping roll (also piked
  roll)

E6 Lifting into handstand
- from angle support/angle
  support with legs astride/free
  pointed angle support
  on the floor

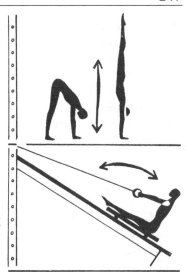

E7 Opening of the arm/trunk angle
- quick and vigorous action at the rolling
  board and wall bars - with ring ropes
  from seated position into supine
  position

E8 Double leg circles
• on a special gymnastic apparatus

E9 Opening of the leg/trunk angle
• quick and vigorous action on the
  buck and wall bar in prone position
• without additional load
• with light additional load
  fastened behind thigh

E10 Leg undercuts, sideways,
- vigorous action into hold position
- with different amplitudes
  from front or reverse standing
  at the bar (wall bars), also free
  standing

IX. Circuit training for strength sports: intensive and extensive interval methods

E1 Clean and jerk
- cleaning with/without squat or using split technique

E2 Squats
- from a 90° knee bent angle position
- with barbell behind neck
- also seated on chair

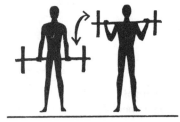

E3 Arm flexion
- under-grip
• in standing position
• in seated position

E4 One-legged squat
- free standing/seated on a chair or medicine ball
- alternating left/right
• with/without additional load

E5 Bench press
- in supine position on the bench

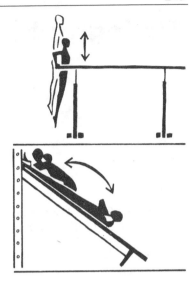

E6 Dips
- on parallel bars or between
  chairs

E7 Sit-ups
- with the trunk
  from inclined lying hang
- with sandbag behind neck
- without sandbag

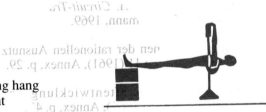

E8 Chin-ups
- in stretch hang or lying hang
- with additional weight

E9 Lateral raises
- arms stretched out at sides
  at shoulder level, raising arms
  up above head in supine position
- with dumbbells/weights/round
  weights/shots

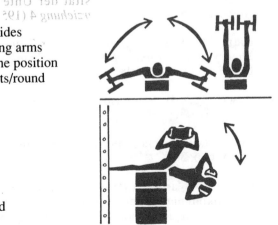

E10 Trunk lifts
- with left/right turn
- without additional load
- with additional load

Bibliography

1. Bernien, E. Die körperliche Grundausbilding an unserer erweiteten Oberschule. In: *Körpererziehung* 12 (1962) 11, p. 571.

2. Bykow, K.M. *Lehrbuch der Physiologie*. Berlin, Volk und Gesundheit, 1960.

3. Dassel, H. and Haag, H. *Circuit-Training in der Schule*. Schorndorf bei Stuttgart, K. Hoffmann, 1969.

4. Dietrich, W. Formen der rationellen Ausnutzung der Unterrichtszeit. In: *Körpererziehung* 11 (1961), Annex, p. 29.

5. Etzold, R. Zur Kraftentwicklung im Turnunterricht. In: *Körpererziehung* 11 (1961), Annex, p. 40.

6. Gugin, A. Über die Intensität der Unterrichtsstunde im Fach Körpererziehung. In: *Körpererziehung* 4 (1954) 11, p. 553.

7. Harre, D., et al. *Principles of Sports Training - Introduction to the Theory and Methods of Training*. (Translation from the German) Berlin, Sportverlag, 1982.

8. Hasenkrüger, H. Stationsbetrieb - Kreisbetrieb. In: *Körpererziehung* 13 (1963) 7/8, p. 365.

9. Heuchert, R. Eine neue Form der Erwärmung. In: *Körpererziehung* 13 (1963) 6, p. 301.

10. Hunold A. and Hoffman, G. Grundformen des Übens zur Vervollkommnung der Bewegungseigenschaften unter dem Aspekt der Belastung und Erholung. In: *Körpererziehung* 13 (1963) 9, p. 445.

11. Israel, S. *Sport, Herzgröße und Herz-Kreislauf-Dynamik.* Leipzig, DHfK, 1967.

12. Jakowlew, N.N. *Biochemie des Sports* (Translation from the Russian). Liepzig, DHfK, 1967.

13. Jonath, U. *Circuit-Training.* Berlin, Limpert, 1961.

14. Kaden, R. Stationsbetrieb im Training. In: *Körpererziehung* 13 (1963) 6, p. 317.

15. Keul, A. and Doll, R. *Muskelstoffwechsel.* München, Barth, 1969.

16. Krestownikow, A.N. *Physiologie der Körperübungen.* (Translation from the Russian) Berlin, Volk und Gesundheit, 1953.

17. Kusnezow, W.W. *Kraftvorbereitung. Theoretische Grundlagen der Muskelkraftentwicklung.* (Translation from the Russian) Berlin, Sportverlag, 1972.

18. Meinel, K. *Bewegungslehre.* 6th ed., Berlin, Volk und Wissen, 1977.

19. Mellerowicz, H. Vergleichende Untersuchungen zur Leistungsentwicklung des Jugendlichen. In: *Leichtathletik* 11 (1960) 235, Annex.

20. Morgan, R.E. and Adamson, G.T. *Circuit Training.* London, Bell & Sons, 1958.

21. Nett, T and Jonath, U. *Kraftübungen zur Konditionsarbeit.* Berlin, Bartels, 1960.

22. Osolin, N.G. *Das Training des Leichtathleten.* (Translation from the Russian) 2nd Ed., Berlin, Sportverlag, 1954.

23. Reimann, R. Für eine allseitige körperliche Grundausbildung. In: *Körpererziehung* 13 (1963) 9, p. 434.

24. Reindell, H. *Herz-Kreislauf-Erkrankungen und Sport.* München, Barth, 1960.

25. Roman, R.A. Die Veränderung der Muskelkraft beim Gewichtheben. In: *Theorie und Praxis der Körperkultur* 8 (1959) 11, p. 1023.

26 Schmolinsky,G., et al. *Track and Field.* (Translation from the German) 2nd ed., Berlin, Sportverlag, 1983.

27. Scholich, M., Löffler, P. and Hendel, H. Zur Entwicklung der Ausdauerfähigkeit im leichtathletischen Grundlagentraining. In: *Der Leichtathlet* 37/1975, 39/1975, 41/1975.

28. Simkin, N.W. *Physiologische Charakteristik von Kraft, Schnelligkeit und Ausdauer.* (Translation from the Russian) Berlin, Sportverlag, 1959.

29. Stemmler, R. Zum Zehnertest als Teil der Abschlußprüfung. In: *Körpererziehung* 13 (1963) 3.

30. Stiehler, G. Zur methodisch-organisatorischen Gestaltung des Sportunterrichts. In: *Theorie und Praxis der Körperkultur* 12 (1963) 8, p. 714.

31. Theiß, G. Die allseitige körperliche Grundausbildung steht im Vordergrund des Turnunterrichts. In: *Körpererziehung* 3 (1963) 5, p. 225.

32. Thieß,G., Schnabel, G., Baumann, R. and et al. *Training von A bis Z. Kleines Wörterbuch für die Theorie und Praxis des sportlichen Trainings.* 2nd ed., Berlin, Sportverlag, 1980.

33. Verchosanskij, J.V. *Grundlagen des speziellen Krafttrainings im Sport.* (Translation from the Russian) In: *Theorie und Praxis der Körperkultur,* 1971, Supplement No. 3, p. 13.

34. Zaciorskij, V.M. Die körperlichen Eigenschaften des Sportlers. In: *Theorie und Praxis der Körperkultur,* 1968, Supplement.

Notes

Notes